GW00630952

# AMERICAN FOOTBALL

## The Skills of the Game

# AMERICAN FOOTBALL

## The Skills of the Game

### LES WILSON

THE CROWOOD PRESS

First published in 1988 by
THE CROWOOD PRESS
Ramsbury, Marlborough
Wiltshire SN8 2HE

© Les Wilson 1988

Paperback edition 1989

All rights reserved. No part of this publication may be reproduced or
transmitted in any form or by any means, electronic or mechanical,
including photocopy, recording, or any information storage and
retrieval system without permission in writing from the publishers.

British Library Cataloguing in Publication Data

Wilson, Les
  American football : the skills of the game.
  1. Football
  I. Title
  769.332      GV951

  ISBN  1  85223  101  7  (HB)
        1  85223  223  4  (PB)

**Dedicated to my parents**

**Acknowledgements**
Thanks to Paula Briatore for typing, Steve Matchett for proof reading,
Dave Parsons for encouragements and Cliff Strougther for showing us
how it's done.
Figs 61, 69, 71, 73, 82, 83, 91, 97, 103, 104, 113, 130, 132 and 133
courtesy of All-Sport Photographic Ltd. All other photographs by
Graham Flewitt.
Line illustrations by Vanetta Joffe.
Cover photographs courtesy of All-Sport Photographic Ltd.

Typeset by Inforum Ltd, Portsmouth
Printed in Great Britain at the University Printing House, Oxford

# Contents

Les Wilson has been involved with American football since its first appearance in the UK. He was assistant coach to the Nottingham Hoods for three years before becoming Head Coach. He is a member of the British Football Coaches Association, and holds regular coaching clinics in the Midlands.

This book is very well done, and should prove to be valuable reading for any potential player. Les Wilson has a tremendous grasp of American football and has expressed his knowledge superbly, in a book which is a must for all aspiring American footballers. Great job!

Dave Kocurek
Pro footballer and coach

The only way that American football is going to grow is through the youth – this book is really going to assist the young player.

Eddie Mitchel
President, 'Football The American Way'

# 1  Fundamentals

## PLAYING AMERICAN FOOTBALL

### Background

Football has been part of the British way of life for several centuries now. In that time it has evolved into many different forms and spread to many different countries. The game as governed by the Football Association is still the purest form of football, but ever since William Webb Ellis picked up a ball and ran with it at Rugby School, the handling codes have gained in popularity.

There are now two different versions of the game of rugby, Rugby League and Rugby Union. These were exported and other nations developed their own variants: Gaelic football in Ireland; the 'Australian rules' game; and American football.

Since American football originated in the 1880s there has been much fine tuning to the game, often to cut down the injuries sustained in what is the toughest team sport in the world. The forward pass was introduced in 1906 as an alternative offense to running with the ball. It was quite a while before the potential of the forward pass was realised, as the macho men of the college circuit considered it 'sissy' and 'cowardly'. Unlimited substitution is now allowed and this has led to the two-platoon game – it is unusual nowadays for a player to play on both offense and defense. In football's early days, a player would be expected to stay on the field for the entire game. Now, if you pick up a knock or a strain, you can leave the field without leaving your team short, and re-enter the fray after treatment.

### Teams

American football is played by two teams of eleven players each, the same as Association Football – and that is where the similarity ends. The unlimited substitution rule means that teams will carry large squads of players. In the National Football League there is a maximum of forty-five players in a squad but in college and British rules there is no limit at all. It is not uncommon for fifty or sixty players to be fully kitted and ready to play.

One of the teams is given the ball and is allowed four attempts (or downs) to advance it ten or more yards. This team is known as the offense. Their opponents will do their best to prevent them gaining these yards. They are known as the defense.

If the offense succeeds in moving the ball ten or more yards, they are allowed another four downs. If they fail to make ten yards, they lose possession, their opponents are given the ball and the roles reverse. The team on the offense becomes the defense, and the team on the defense becomes the offense. It is quite unusual for a player to play on both offense and defense, so a change of possession normally sees twenty-two players leave the field to be replaced by another twenty-two.

### Advancing the Ball

There are two ways the offense can move the ball. They can run with it or they can pass it. Whatever method they choose, every play begins with the snap. This involves a player (the center) handing the ball between his legs

# Fundamentals

to the quarterback. The quarterback will then either hand the ball to a running back, or pass the ball forward to one of his receivers.

Whilst the offense are doing this, the defense will attempt to gain possession of the ball. They will tackle the ball carrier or receiver to minimise any yardage gain or, even better, cause the ball carrier to drop (or fumble) the ball or intercept a pass. If the ball goes out of bounds, it remains in the possession of the offense.

## Goal-kick

If, after three of their four allotted downs, the offense feel they will not make the necessary ten yards, they may decide to kick the ball. If a team is within thirty or forty yards of their opponents' endzone they will probably elect to kick a field goal. This involves snapping the ball to a point at least seven yards behind the line of scrimmage, placing it on the ground and then kicking it between the goal-posts. If they are successful, they score three points. If they miss, the opposition gains possession at the point of the snap.

## Punting

If they are out of field goal range, the offense will punt the ball deep into their opponents' territory. This is a kick, made at least twelve yards behind the line of scrimmage, of a ball that is in the air. The defense can either let the ball come to rest and gain possession at that point, or they can catch the punt and run the ball back at the offense. They then begin their four attempts to move the ball ten yards.

## Scoring

The aim of the game is to score more points than your opponents. One method of scoring is the field goal, which is worth three points.

The other main method of scoring is a touchdown, worth six points. This is awarded when a runner with the ball crosses or touches his opponents' goal line, or when a player catches a pass or recovers a loose ball within his opponents' endzone.

Any side which scores a touchdown is allowed to add to that score by either kicking the ball between the goal posts for one extra point, or by running or passing the ball into the endzone for two extra points. (In the NFL only one point is given for either method.) These extra point attempts take place from the 3-yard line (2-yard line in the NFL).

Play after any score is restarted by the scoring side kicking the ball from the 35-yard line into their opponents' half. The one exception to this rule is in the event of a safety score. This is when an offensive ball carrier is tackled in his own endzone. The defending side is then awarded two points and the offense has to kick-off from its own 20-yard line. So a side conceding a safety is penalised twice – they concede points and they lose possession.

## Duration

The duration of a game is sixty minutes which is divided into two halves. Between the halves there is a twenty-minute break to allow the teams to rest and to discuss their strategy. Each half is divided into two fifteen-minute quarters and at the end of the game's first and third quarters the two teams will change ends.

The game clock does not run continuously but is stopped every time the ball goes out of bounds, when a pass is not caught, when a team scores or when the officials award a penalty. Each team is also allowed to stop the clock three times in each half and the officials will call *time out* whenever they feel it is necessary, such as for the treatment of injured players. The game clock is also stopped two minutes before the end of each half, which is known as *the two-minute warning*. This continual stopping and starting of the game clock means that the average sixty-minute football game will actually last between two-and-a-half and three hours.

# Rules

As with any sport there is a set of rules telling you what you can and cannot do. The rules of American Football run to some ninety pages and are enforced by a team of five officials (seven in the NFL), who are dressed in black and white striped shirts and wear white caps. The head official is called the referee and he is easy to identify because he wears a black cap.

The officials use a whistle to signal the start and finish of a play but not to signal a penalty. If an official spots an infraction of the rules he identifies the spot with a yellow marker called a flag. The referee then offers the offended team's captain several options, most of which involve moving the ball back five, ten or fifteen yards depending on the severity of the foul.

If the offense commits a serious foul it could find itself with twenty-five yards to make in four downs instead of ten yards. Similarly, if the defense commits a serious infraction the offense could be moved forwards fifteen yards which would take them over the ten yards needed and they would be awarded another four downs.

# Equipment *(Fig 1)*

The most visible change has been in the amount of protective equipment used by the

KEY

OFFENSIVE PLAYERS

○     linemen (tackles, guards, ends)
       backs
       receivers

⊗     center

DEFENSIVE PLAYERS

✕     secondary (safeties, cornerbacks)

▽     linebackers (outside linebackers, middle linebackers)

☐     linemen (ends, tackles)

• • • • •     ball being carried

– – – –     ball in the air

〰〰     motion

≢     hand off

Shoulder pads

Spine pad
(behind)

Helmet, facecage
and mouth guard

Hip pads

Thigh pads

Knee pads

Fig 1    Certain items of kit are required by the rules of the game.

players. Knee pads, thigh pads, shoulder pads and helmets have turned the American footballer into a modern day knight in armour. If you are going to play football, it is essential that you know what equipment is compulsory and the right way to wear it.

Rule 1 of the British American football rules lists the following mandatory equipment, which must be professionally manufactured and not altered to decrease protection: knee pads; thigh pads; hip pads; tailbone protector (spine pad); shoulder pads; head protector (helmet) with a four-point chin-strap; intra-oral mouthpiece (gum shield).

The helmet is the most vital piece of your equipment so make sure it is in good order. It must be of a type approved by the American organisation NOCSAE (National Operation Committee on Standards for Athletic Equipment), and must carry a label stating this. It is fitted with air pockets and must be correctly inflated so that it fits tightly, but comfortably, all over your head, and does not move about. The face cage should be firmly secured and be strong enough to stand up to the hardest collisions. The gum shield is also a very important piece of kit. Although it will help protect your teeth, its main purpose is to prevent concussion caused by your lower jaw hitting your upper jaw when you take a big hit. The gum shield can be a bit uncomfortable if you are not used to wearing it, but resist the temptation to trim the ends off – apart from reducing the protection, it is illegal. Rule 1 states that the mouth guard must cover *all* your upper teeth.

There is more equipment that you can wear if you so wish, although you are not required to by law. An abdominal protector (box) similar to that worn by cricketers is popular with many players (for obvious reasons), as are soccer players' shin pads. Rib pads are quite an asset to those players who are unable to protect themselves. Players such as quarter-

backs, receivers, punters and kickers have to do their jobs and take the hits as they come, so they tend to wear more padding than the others. Linemen and linebackers like to wear neck-rolls, which help prevent neck injuries, and forearm pads to prevent bruising on the arms. Go into any equipment shop and you will see shelves full of protective equipment. What you wear is up to you, but if you feel you need something, then wear it. Don't be put off by the jibes of your team-mates. If it gives you confidence then it can only do you good.

A final word on protective equipment: it is just that – protective. Your helmet is not designed as a weapon and it is illegal to use it as such. Every helmet carries a warning stating that it must not be used to butt, ram or spear an opponent and the rules state that it must not be the main point of contact in blocking or tackling. The game is tough enough without people deliberately trying to cripple each other.

## The Field *(Fig 2)*

The American football pitch, or field as it is called, is 100 yards long and 53 yards 1 foot wide. At each end of this area is a 10-yard long endzone. If you are used to playing on a rugby or soccer pitch, the first thing you will notice is that the American football field is very narrow. This makes outside runs very difficult, as the sweeping back runs into the sideline before he can outstrip the defense.

The goal-posts are set right at the back of the endzone, not on the goal-line as in rugby football. So if the kicker is on the 20-yard line, he has a 30-yard kick to score. The goal-posts are narrower than in rugby football, being only 18 feet 6 inches apart, although the cross bar is the same height, at 10 feet above the ground. As the ball is also smaller than a rugby ball, it is not as easy to kick a long range field goal as you might think.

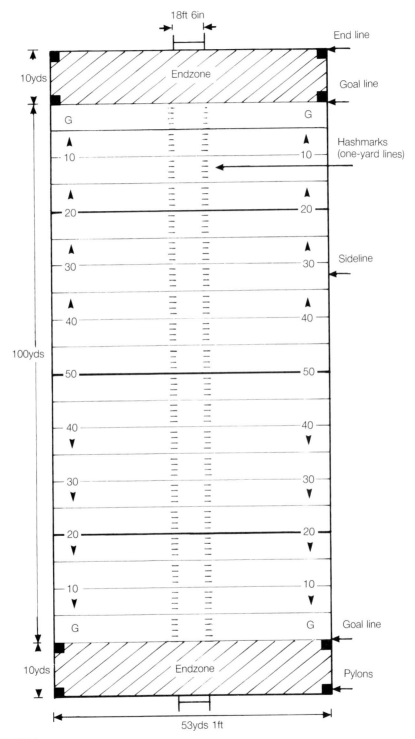

*Fig 2    The football field.*

If you are new to American football you will find many new techniques in this book. Some of them may feel awkward at first but persevere and they will become as natural as kicking a soccer ball. The important thing is to get it right straight from the word go. Don't cheat yourself: it is much harder to forget an incorrect technique than to learn a new one from scratch.

# FITNESS

Football is a sport which demands an all-round fitness and athleticism. Television and the Press have made such a great fuss about the giants of the game that the general public think that you cannot possibly play ball unless you are over 6 feet 4 inches and weigh at least 18 stone. People of *all* sizes can find a position to fill, provided they are fit. It is no use being that 6 foot 4 inch, 18-stone Goliath, if your time for the 40-yard dash is 8 seconds. Your waist measurement must be less than your chest measurement!

Don't be put off if you are out of condition at the moment. All it takes is dedication and time. If you really want to *play* football (and not just pose in the kit), then you *will* play football. It's up to you.

Fitness consists of four major components: strength, speed, stamina and flexibility. All of these are needed if you are to play football well and escape injury. The body takes an exceptional pounding during a game and you should not consider playing unless you are confident about your fitness.

## Warm-Up *(Figs 3 to 7)*

Before commencing any physical activity it is essential to warm up. When the body is warm it functions at its best. If you do not warm up properly you are likely to pull muscles.

You must set aside fifteen minutes to warm up in warm weather and at least half an hour during the winter. It is no good jogging a length of the field just before kick-off and expecting to compete with a team that is already on the boil. As well as preventing injury, warming up will probably stop you conceding a couple of early touchdowns.

Start your session by jogging a couple of laps of the field at a steady pace, to loosen the leg muscles and set the cardio-vascular system pumping. Players should then line up in regular rows and columns, about five yards from each other. From the beginning, emphasis should be placed on discipline and teamwork. All exercises should be carried out together and in unison. Stretching should be done gently and smoothly, without bouncing. Stretch until you feel the muscle pulling, hold for fifteen seconds and then relax. Do not over-stretch yourself. It helps to breathe out whilst stretching and this can be achieved by counting the seconds out loud. Repeat each exercise three times.

1.   *Calf stretch* This stretches the calf muscles of the rear leg. Ensure that the rear heel is kept on the floor and the foot pointing straight forwards. Keep your body upright and push your hips forwards, bending your front knee. Repeat the exercise with the other leg to the rear.

2.   *Jack-knife stretch* Put your feet together, keep your back and legs straight, and bend at the hips until you feel a pull in your hamstrings. Do not force this stretch if you feel pain in your lower back.

3.   *Way-backs* With your hands behind your helmet, press your shoulders and elbows backwards. This stretches shoulder and upper back muscles.

4.   *Groin stretch* Keeping your feet wide apart and your body upright, bend one leg, putting your weight on the other leg. This will

Fig 3    Calf stretch.

Fig 4    Jack-knife.

Fig 5    Groin stretch.

stretch the groin muscles of the straight leg. Hold for fifteen seconds and then transfer your weight to the other leg.

5.   *Hurdle stretch* With your left leg forward and your right leg back, try to put your head on the knee of the straight leg, whilst keeping your back straight. Hold for fifteen seconds once you feel a pull behind the knee, and then lean back until your shoulders are on the floor. Keep your left leg straight and your right knee as near to the floor as you can. Hold for a further fifteen seconds. Repeat with alternate legs. This will stretch the hamstrings, quadriceps and groin.

6.   *Back stretch* Lying on your back, swing your feet over your head and attempt to touch the floor. Keep your legs and back straight and support yourself with your hands on your hips. Hold for fifteen seconds and then carefully lower your feet to the floor. This is a good exercise for stretching back and hamstring muscles. However, it is possible to tear lower back muscles if you return to the start position too violently, so be careful.

7.   *Star jumps (Jumping Jacks)* About twenty or thirty star jumps will loosen up the arm and leg joints.

8.   *Sprints* Finish the warm-up with six forty-yard sprints. The first two sprints should be done at half pace, the next two at three-quarter pace and the final two at full pace.

## Strength *(Figs 8 to 11)*

The best way to improve your strength is to participate in a supervised weight-training programme. The programme should be planned to develop muscles without reducing your speed and reflexes. Whilst the upper body must not be neglected, most exercises should

*Fig 6   Hurdle stretch.*

*Fig 7  Back stretch.*

be geared to the legs, neck, shoulders and triceps.

The initial reaction of new players is to want to increase weight. I would not recommend this as it can slow you down and reduce your endurance. You should only attempt to put on weight if your body frame can cope with it.

The following exercises will help to build strength but are no substitute for weight-training:

1.  *Push-ups* From front support position, lower your chest to the floor by bending your arms. Keep the body straight. Return to front support position by straightening your arms.
2.  *Sit-ups* Lie on your back and place your middle fingers in the ear-holes of your helmet. Bend your knees. From this position, raise your elbows to touch your knees and return.
3.  *Mountain climbers* In front support position, move one leg forwards to assume track sprint stance. Keeping your hands on the floor, alternate your feet as fast as possible.
4.  *Extension push-ups* This is the same as a normal push-up, except that your arms and legs are spread as wide as possible.
5.  *Squat thrusts* Front support position again. Keeping your hands on the floor, jump both feet as far forwards as possible and then jump back.
6.  *Four-man push-ups* Four players form a square in front support position with their feet across one another. At a given signal, all players push up. Hold for ten seconds and lower.

Fig 8    Push-ups.

Fig 9    Sit-ups.

Fig 10    Mountain climbers.

Fig 11    Four-man push-ups — these build strength and team-work.

## **Speed** *(Fig 12)*

Football is an explosive sport. Most plays involve running only five or ten yards at a time, with forty yards generally being considered the longest distance run during the average down. Most coaches time their players over forty yards and this is a good indication of their speed. The ability to hit top speed after only two or three paces is essential.

Many people think that you cannot improve your speed. This is, of course, not true. You need to work on your technique – it is surprising how many people do not know how to run properly. Time should be allocated at *every*

*Fig 12    Good sprinting style – high knees, pumping arms and forward lean.*

training session for work on sprinting speed and technique – it is that important.

There are several points to remember when running:

1.    Keep all your limbs moving straight forwards. This may sound obvious, but a quick look at most amateur sportsmen will show that arms and legs tend to fly in all directions. Keep your arms pumping forward and back, and not from side to side. Your hands should move from your waist up to the level of your chin and back again.

2.    Lift your knee high as you move it forwards. This will lengthen your stride.

3.    Lean slightly forwards. This will be discussed in more detail under running back techniques.

4.    Push off hard, run on your toes and drive your foot into the ground. The calf muscle is under-utilised by most people who are considered slow runners. Pushing off hard with the foot takes time and practice to perfect, but is the biggest single factor in increasing speed.

5.    After you have worked on your technique, learn to relax. By unclenching your hands and not gritting your teeth it is possible to gain a yard on your forty-yard dash.

The best way to improve your sprinting is to sprint. Always finish each training session with a few sprints, remembering to concentrate on technique. A good schedule is four five-yard sprints, four ten-yard sprints, two twenty-yard sprints and finally two forty-yard sprints. Allow ten yards to slow down after each run, even the five-yard sprints. These shortest runs are to improve your acceleration and you should be at top speed at the end of the distance.

To make sprint training more interesting, there are several drills you can utilise:

1.    *Pass routes* Practise running long routes whilst a quarterback throws the ball to you.

2. *'Cover the pastures'* Player A stands center field on the 40-yard line, facing the near endzone. Player B stands facing him on the 30-yard line. Player A has to get into the endzone without being caught by Player B.

3. *'Head 'em off at the pass'* This is similar to the previous drill. Player B is still center field on the 30-yard line. Player A is on the 40-yard line but only 15 yards from the sideline. This will also teach Player B to judge his angle of pursuit as he attempts to intercept Player A before he reaches the endzone.

## Stamina

Stamina is the measure of your ability to last the pace. It is no use playing well for most of the game, only to see the opposition overtake you in the fourth quarter because you have run out of steam.

There are two kinds of stamina which have to be developed: muscular stamina and cardio-vascular stamina. Muscular stamina can be increased by doing the exercises listed in the strength and speed sections.

Cardio-vascular stamina is best improved by distance running. As football is a short-distance sport, huge marathon runs are not necessary. Rather, you should run about one to one-and-a-half miles at a time. Do this twice a week and time yourself. You should see a steady improvement in your times. Once you can regularly run one-and-a-half miles in under eleven minutes you should vary your schedule. On one day, aim for as fast a time as possible. On another, change pace during the run, for example jog one hundred yards, then sprint fifty yards. (This mixed-speed running goes by the delightful name of fartlek.)

## Flexibility

This concerns the ability to move the joints to their full limits. Good flexibility will help you

move better on the field, but more importantly it will prevent the sprains and twists that can occur during the season. To improve flexibility, repeat the stretches given in the warm-up section. Make sure you have warmed up well and then do your stretches. This time hold the stretch for about thirty seconds. Remember not to bounce. Repeat each exercise three times, and by the third repetition you should be stretching further before you feel it pulling.

## Agility *(Fig 13)*

Although not strictly a component of your fitness, it is important to be agile. Fast feet are important in all positions, not least of all on the line. You need to be able to dodge between people and to step over fallen bodies. The following exercises are good aids to agility:

1. *Skipping* The good old-fashioned child's skipping rope is an excellent way to speed up your footwork. World champion boxers use it, so why shouldn't you?

2. *Railroad* Players line up in single file. Player A lies face down on the floor. Player B runs over him and lies down one yard further on. Player C runs over the first two and then lies down. This continues until all players are lying down. Player A then stands up and runs over all the others. After he has passed over Player B, Player B gets up and follows him. The 'railroad' should be moving along on its own. Remember to pick your feet up when you are running and make sure you do not tread on any of your team-mates – you will not be very popular if you do.

3. *Carioca* This is a sideways shuffle step. The trailing leg alternately crosses over in front of the leading leg and then behind it. Carioca a length of the pitch facing inwards, and then return facing the same direction.

4. *Chopping* This is the archetypal football exercise, but it is useful for all fast ball games.

Fig 13  Railroad – keep your feet high.

Assume the base position (as described later in this chapter) and then run on the spot keeping your feet shoulder-width apart. The aim is to move your feet as quickly as possible.

During the action of a game, players should never be still. If they chop whilst reading the play, their speed off the mark will be quicker. (Watch tennis players waiting for the ball to be returned.) A good drill for practising this is called 'breakdowns'. Players commence a forty-yard sprint. On a whistle from the coach they stop running and chop on the spot. On a second whistle they drop to the floor, then stand up and sprint through to the end. This drill develops stamina as well as agility.

## THE POSITIONS

Once you are fit, you will want to begin playing. The first question you will ask is, 'What position should I play?' As a beginner to the game you should attempt to play in every possible position. This has many advantages. Firstly, you will appreciate what your team-mates have to do during each play. Secondly, you will gain knowledge to help in your final chosen position. Thirdly, you are more likely to get more playing time during a game – coaches like versatile players.

## Offense *(Fig 14)*

### *Wide Receiver*

He must be able to catch! This is often forgotten when people opt to play here. This means more than catching a simple lobbed pass in practice, he must be prepared to dive full length to catch a bullet pass thrown into a group of several mean defenders. As a bonus, he should be fast and have excellent moves (agility).

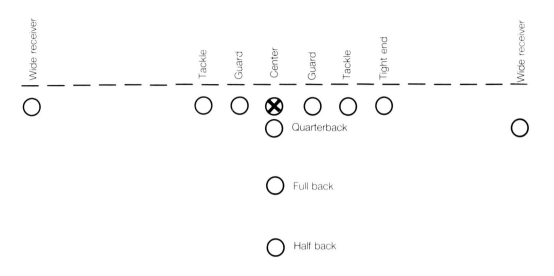

*Fig 14    Offense (I-formation).*

## Tackles

These are normally the biggest and strongest men on the offense. They must be able to block any defender in a one-on-one situation, yet must be agile enough to drop back and pass block.

## Guard

Guards are the fastest of the interior linemen. Size and strength are not as important as speed and a willingness to hit hard. (A pulling guard is required to beat his running back to the hole.)

## Center

The most important man on the offense. If he fouls up, it is no good having John Elway or Walter Payton in the backfield. He must be extremely agile, to be able to snap the ball back and then block the nose tackle.

## Tight End

The tight end has to be the most versatile player on the offensive line. Not only does he have to block like a tackle, but he has to catch like a wide receiver and run like a full back. Size and speed are probably more important than strength.

## Quarterback

He must be able to run as well as pass. His mental capabilities are as important as his physical attributes. He is the leader of the offense and must act as such – he must never lose his cool, even under the most intense intimidation.

## Full Back

He is normally the biggest and strongest of the backs. He is expected to gain ground in short yardage situations as well as blocking for the

# Fundamentals

half back. If he is speedy, he can also be used as ball carrier on wide plays.

## Half Back

Size is not so important here. The half back must have great speed and agility to run wide yet have the toughness to run up the middle. He will have to block and catch passes, but if he can pass the ball as well, it will add a surprise element to the offense.

# Defense *(Fig 15)*

## Ends

These are normally the fastest of the defensive linemen. They must take on the offensive tackle to the inside, yet move outside on wide runs. Size and strength are crucial.

## Tackles

The strongest defenders. They have to stop inside runs, often against double team blocking. They must also be able to rush the quarterback with pace.

## Linebackers

These are the outside linebackers (OLB) and the middle linebackers (MLB). They must be quick, agile and tough. They must be sure tacklers and be able to play pass defense. They must also be intelligent enough to read each play as it develops.

## The Secondary

The secondary consists of cornerbacks (CB), strong safety (SS), and free safety (FS). Speed

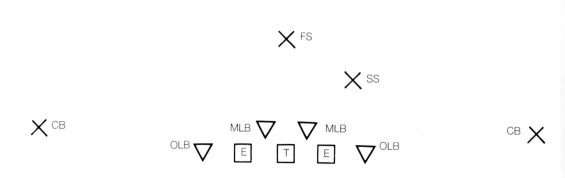

*Fig 15   Defense (52-formation).*

is more important than size in the secondary. The cornerbacks are usually the fastest men in a squad. They have to be able to turn and catch wide receivers who will normally have one or two yards' start on them. Everybody in the secondary must be a sure tackler as they are usually the last line of defense. If the offense gets past the safeties, they should score.

## Special Teams

Most of the players on special teams are drawn from the regular offensive and defensive units. However, kickers are normally a specialised position.

Anybody can play kicker or punter. Size and speed are not important, as what is needed is a good temperament and consistency. The punter needs to be able to kick long and high, but surprisingly, distance is not too crucial for the goal kicker. If you can guarantee consistent kicks from within thirty-five yards of the goal, then you will probably be first choice kicker for your team. Strong leg muscles are an asset, but all kicking is more a question of technique and timing.

## THE BASE *(Figs 16 & 17)*

'Football', said Vince Lombardi, 'is not a contact sport, it is a collision sport.' Vince Lombardi was reckoned to be the greatest of all football coaches and many of his sayings are passed down to today's coaches and players. 'If you want a contact sport', he said, 'take up ballroom dancing!'

To cope with the continual collisions during a game, you must have a good base. The base position is often referred to by other names: the hitting position, the linebacker

Fig 16    The base position. The most fundamental of all football techniques.

Fig 17    The base position – side view.

# Fundamentals

stance, or the two-point stance. Whichever name you choose, it is essential to every player, being the position you assume just prior to making contact with an opponent. Linebackers and the secondary line up in this position to be ready for the first tackle. It is so important, that the first thing I do at *every* training session is to get all the players into the base position. I shout '*hit*', and the players assume the position and stay there until they are told to come up. This hit drill is repeated several times during a session. It is also good for improving reaction times.

Stand with your feet just over shoulder-width apart and turn them so that they are parallel and pointing straight forwards. Squat down, keeping your back straight and not bending at the waist. In this position you are ready to use all your muscles to explode towards your opponent. Most important of all – *keep your head up*. This means keep it pulled back against your shoulders, with your neck muscles bunched up behind it. If you drop your head you will not be able to see, and you also risk serious injury to your spine.

Whenever you are on a football pitch – *keep your head up*. If there is one phrase that I have to say more often than any other during a season it is *keep your head up*.

# 2 Offensive Techniques

## THE OFFENSIVE LINE

Talk to most spectators about building an offense and they will either mention running backs or quarterbacks. Ask any coach and he will tell you, 'You must have a good line'.

The interior line is the heart of any offense, yet it is often difficult to persuade newcomers to play there. The glory is all on the defense, where due credit is given for your tackles. On the offensive line, you take on twenty-stone players, clearing the way for your running back to stroll into the endzone untouched, and everybody ignores you. They all rush over to the scorer who has probably not even broken sweat!

Another problem with playing on the offensive line is the amount of unjust criticism you can pick up. It needs all five members of the line to block correctly. If just one member fouls up, the play is broken and your own supreme effort is unnoticed as the whole line is castigated by the coach and fans. If you only play for the glory, the offensive line is not for you.

Fortunately, there are enough selfless people in most squads to build a dedicated line. Control the line of scrimmage and you control the game.

## Three-Point Stance (Fig 18)

We have already covered the two-point stance in Chapter 1. The three-point stance is an exension of the two-point and is used by the offensive line and running backs. It has been developed to give you the best all-round start to a play, whether you are driving, pulling or pass blocking. By using the same three-point stance on every down you will not tip the play to the defense.

Work hard on achieving a good stance – you can practise it at home in front of a mirror. If your stance is flawed you will either be too upright and not able to block effectively, or you will be too slow out of your blocks. The motto of an offensive line could be 'Hit hard – Hit fast' and a good stance will help you achieve this.

Take up the base position, but with your right foot (if you are right-handed) a few inches back. Lean forwards and place your right hand on the ground in line with your right knee. Your back and shoulders should be parallel with the floor. *Keep your head up*. Most of your weight should be on your feet so that if your hand is knocked away, you will not fall over.

In the initial stages, you should always move into your stance in three distinct phases:

1. Feet in correct position.
2. Squat down into base position.
3. Place hand on floor.

After a while you will find that you combine all three steps into a continuous smooth action.

Once you have taken up your three-point you need to be able to move out of it properly: power off with all your leg muscles; push hard with your feet; stay low. The biggest fault with beginners is the tendency to stand up before moving forward. Pump your arms hard and *keep your head up*. You want to see where you're going, don't you?

# Offensive Techniques

Fig 18   The three-point stance.

## Blocking

The *raison d'être* of the offensive line is to keep the defense from their backs. They do this by blocking. There are quite a few types of block, but we will only discuss the basic ones. All other blocks you may come across are variations of these.

### Drive Block (Fig 19)

The basic drive block requires you to drive your shoulder into the defender's belt buckle. Step with your right foot as you hit him with your right shoulder. You need to get under him to push him off balance. Remember that the laws of the game require you to keep your hands within the framework of his body, and not to hold.

The principle of the drive block is the same as that of the assegai. This is a short spear used for stabbing – the Zulu warrior would attempt to drive it upwards into the enemy's stomach, and out between his shoulder-blades. This rather gory example indicates the angle at which you should attack the defender. Drive up through him, keep your legs moving (and shoulder-width apart) and you'll find you can move him where you want.

The initial tendency is to make the first hit and then stop. This allows the defender to regroup and charge again. Once you have got him, you must keep going. Never give a loser a second chance.

Fig 19    Drive blocking – keep your feet moving.

## Cut Block (Fig 20)

There are times when it is not necessary to drive your opponent out of the way of a running back, just to delay him from reaching the action. For instance, if you are playing left tackle and the play is wide to the right, you will not achieve anything by drive blocking your opponent, as his assignment would be to leave your area and take an angle of pursuit. To prevent him doing this you will have to cut him.

Make initial contact as in the drive block. Then, as he rushes into you, drop on to all fours and turn your tail towards him. His momentum will cause him to fall over you. A common mistake is to drop to all fours before making initial contact, which will allow the defender to grab your pads and throw you out

of his way (and leave you looking very silly). Also, stay on all fours until you have completed the block. Linemen should practise crawling until it becomes a natural movement.

## Double Team Block (Fig 21)

This involves two blockers hitting one defender. We will discuss this block assuming we want to force our opponent to the left. The left man is designated the 'post', and the right man, the 'turn'.

The post man drive blocks with his right shoulder. He is only stopping the defender, not driving him. The turn man hits with his left shoulder, just higher than the post man. As soon as the turn man hits, the post man swings his tail to the right and the pair of them drive the defender away. The two blockers

Fig 20    Cut block – stay on all fours so you are still mobile.

Fig 21    Double team block.

*Fig 22   Cross blocking – make sure you know who is going in front.*

must keep tight, as it is possible for the defender to break loose by charging between them.

## Cross Block (Fig 22)

In a cross block, two linemen block each other's opponent. You and your partner have to decide who is going in front of whom, or your coach will tell you.

The first man slants across and makes a drive block with his outside shoulder, making sure his head is *in front* of his man. The second man steps with his near foot towards the spot where the first man lined up. He lets his partner cross him and then drive blocks his opponent out.

If this block is carried out well and infrequently, to gain a surprise element, your backs will have a huge hole to run into.

## Pass Block (Fig 23)

Without doubt the most difficult football technique to teach is pass blocking. In fact, it is probably one of the most difficult techniques of *any* sport.

The actual mechanics of pass blocking are quite simple. Move out of your three-point into the base position. Keep your feet chopping and retreat into the pass pocket. As the defender closes, hit him hard with the heel of your hands by extending your arms and straightening your legs. You must make contact at the bottom of his shoulder pads to gain maximum leverage and knock him back. Then return to the base position and await his next charge.

This may sound easy, but the difficulty is to ensure that you always remain in a straight line between the defender and your quarterback. You must always remain square-on to the defender. If he tries to rush beside you, do not turn your body, but shuffle sideways to maintain your position. Also, be patient: do not rush

Fig 23   Pass blocking – the most difficult of all techniques to master.

after him, let him come to you. If you leave your position in the pocket, you can be sure a linebacker will fire into the gap you have left. Eventually you will have to do something drastic, because you cannot keep retreating and hitting forever. If the defender tries to rush outside, the best thing is to keep him going wide and let his own momentum carry him away. If he moves inside, or attempts to run through you, then you should cut him. Again this uses his momentum to your advantage.

Practise pass blocking with your whole unit. It is important that you know where all your team-mates are, especially the quarterback.

## Blocking Rules

The rules of football concerning offensive blocking are quite strict. They may also vary from league to league, so always check what is and what is not allowed. The two most common penalties conceded by the offensive line are for *holding* and *clipping*.

Holding is just what it says – you must not grab hold of your opponent, and your hands must be within the framework of his body. If they slip round him you will be called for holding and marched back ten yards.

You are only allowed to block from the front, hence, making contact from the side or behind (clipping) is illegal. However, this rule normally only applies down-field. In the vicinity

*Fig 24    Pulling – the player steps in the direction he is pulling.*

of the line of scrimmage, clipping is usually allowed.

## Pulling *(Fig 24)*

Most coaches require their linemen to pull off the line of scrimmage at some time, either to trap a defensive lineman or to lead a play round the end.

To pull out to the right, jab your right elbow into your waist and whip your arm round to the right. At the same time, step to the right with your right foot so that it is at right angles to your left foot. Then sprint along the line of scrimmage. Don't veer towards your backs – remember you have to beat them to the hole, so take the shortest route. Stay low, and as soon as you meet a defender, drop into the

base position and block him. Unless your coach specifically tells you not to, always block the first man you see. If no defender penetrates the backfield, turn up-field as soon as you have passed your tight end. The defense will attempt to string you out towards the sideline for a zero gain, so cut up-field and force a gap for your runners.

## The Center *(Fig 25)*

As I said earlier, the center has a very difficult role to play. Not only must he be able to execute all of the above blocks, but he must snap the ball as well. He uses a normal three-point stance except that his right hand (if right-handed) holds the football. The laces should be to the left so that they hit the

# Offensive Techniques

Fig 25    *The center can use one or two hands to snap the ball.*

quarterback's top hand. Some centers like to place their left elbow on their left knee.

The center must practise snapping with his quarterback until all actions are second nature. He should charge forwards as he snaps the ball. If he snaps without charging, a strong nose tackle will drive him back into the quarterback before he can block. Remember, if the snap fails, the offense fails.

## RECEIVERS

The rules of football say that there must be at least seven men on the line of scrimmage, and that only the two end men may catch a forward pass. Any players at least one yard behind the line of scrimmage may also legally catch a forward pass. In normal offensive formations this means that the five interior linemen (tackles, guards and center) and the quarterback are ineligible receivers. Note, however, that if the quarterback lines up in the shotgun position, he is more than one yard behind the line of scrimmage and therefore makes himself eligible.

Most teams line up with one of the end men close to the tackle. He is called the tight end. The other end man lines up fifteen yards from the ball and is called the split end. If you require a receiver wide out on the tight end's side, he must be at least one yard behind the line. This player is called the flankerback. The split end and the flankerback are generally known as wide receivers.

In NFL football it is increasingly common for

a side to use two split ends and no tight end. Along with two or three flankerbacks the pass-only offense is used on long yardage downs, or when a side is two or three touchdowns behind. In junior football there are usually only one or two wide receivers.

If you play tight end, you should spend most time working on the blocking aspects of the game. There is a tendency amongst newcomers to treat a tight end as a receiver who blocks, when in fact he is a lineman who can catch. Tight ends should use the three-point stance. As your action on the majority of plays will be to block the outside linebacker, you should fake a block on him when you have to run a pattern. The backer will attempt to avoid your block, and leave you a path down-field.

The remainder of this section is aimed at wide receivers, although the notes on pass routes apply to any eligible receiver.

## Stances

There are two types of stance used by wide receivers: the upright and the track stance.

### Upright Stance

This is the easiest stance to assume. Move your outside foot forwards and keep your weight mainly on this front foot. Turn your head to watch the ball. Away from the line it is often difficult to hear the snap count, so if in any doubt, wait until you see the ball snapped.

### Track Stance (Fig 26)

This stance is rarely used in pro football but is often found at high school and college level. It is simply the stance used by the track sprinter, which gives good speed off the mark and also keeps you low. The main reason for its demise at the top level is that you cannot easily see the defense's alignment.

## Blocking

Although your main job as a wide receiver is to catch passes, you must perform a useful function on running plays. The main blocks you will use are the drive block and the cut block. The trick you must learn is not to block too soon, rather you must allow the play to develop and only block your opponent when he is in position to do some damage. If you block him too early, he will recover and go on to make a tackle.

## Moving Off

Sometimes your opponent will hang five yards off you and make it easy for you to move down-field. Often, he will stand right in front of you and try to stop you leaving the line of scrimmage. (Check your league rules for this. Some leagues allow contact only within five yards down-field; others allow contact at any time until the ball is in the air.)

If he does try to stop you, there are two main ways to beat him. The simplest way is to power your way past him. Stay low and hit him with your inside shoulder against his outside hip. The second way is to take a jab step (side-step) in the opposite direction. Then push off hard with that foot and accelerate past him. If you beat him often enough, he will drop back to give himself a chance. It is a great feeling when you know you've got your opponent worried.

## Routes (Fig 27)

A route is just what it says it is: the set of directions you are given to tell you how to get from your starting position to your catching position. By running predetermined routes the quarterback knows exactly where his receivers will be. He can then concentrate on reading the defense before firing his pass.

# Offensive Techniques

Fig 26 Track stance – popular with high schools in the United States but not often seen in Britain.

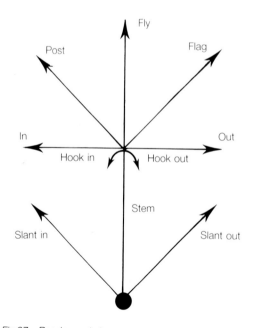

Fig 27 Passing route tree.

When running routes, you have several things to remember. Firstly, run the distance as accurately as possible – if you have a ten-yard hook, make sure you run ten yards and not eight yards or twelve yards. This first part of a route is called the stem. Then you have to change direction. This is known as the cut (not to be confused with the cut block). If your cut is 90 degrees, make it a sharp right angle. Don't round the corner off. Plant your outside foot down hard and push off. You should run the stem of your pattern at about 85 per cent of your top speed, and hit top speed immediately after the cut.

There are as many routes as there are football fans, and your coach will always invent new ones for you. These are a few of the more common ones:

1. *Slant-in/out* Fire out at full speed at a 45-degree angle to the line of scrimmage. If

you are running a slant-in, look for the ball over your inside shoulder. If it is a slant-out, the ball will arrive over your outside shoulder.

2. *Flag* Run your stem and then cut towards the corner flag. Look for the ball over your outside shoulder immediately after your cut.

3. *Post* This is the same as a flag, except the cut is towards the goal post. Look over your inside shoulder for the ball.

4. *Out* Run your stem and then cut at right angles towards the sideline. Look over your outside shoulder and don't stop running until you reach the sideline. Then head up-field.

5. *In* The opposite of an out.

6. *Hook-in/out* Run the stem, then turn sharply and face the quarterback in the base position.

7. *Fly* The pattern for speed merchants! Run as fast as you can and burn off the defender.

The length of a stem will be specified by your coach. When you can run these patterns accurately and consistently, add a little fake before you cut. This could gain you another couple of yards over the covering defender.

## Catching *(Fig 28)*

Having taken up your stance, charged up-field, cut outside and successfully beaten the cornerback, you must catch the football. This is not as simple as it sounds, as it's only when you try it yourself, that you realise how difficult it is to hold on to that piece of pigskin. Learn the correct technique and then practise, practise, practise. Even if it is only throwing the ball to yourself, it will all help to develop sticky fingers.

The golden rule for catching the football is: catch it in your *hands*. If you play soccer or rugby, you will be taught to field the ball by catching it against your chest. If you try that in

*Fig 28    This receiver shows the correct position of the hands prior to receiving a high pass.*

football, with the hard American ball and your rigid pads, the ball will easily bounce away from you. So catch it in your hands: make your fingers and thumbs into a basket and grab the ball. Then put your middle finger over the point of the ball and tuck it under your arm.

Once the ball is in the air, it is literally up for grabs. You, as the receiver, have no automatic right to it, it is as much the defender's ball as it is yours. So always keep your eye on the ball, and don't worry about anything else. Break up your pattern if the ball is badly thrown and catch it at the earliest opportunity. If it is a high pass, jump and catch it high – don't wait for it to come down or it may be intercepted. And don't worry about the cornerback hitting you hard, he'll hit you whether you catch it or not, so you may as well get something out of the play.

## RUNNERS

The running backs are the golden boys of the offense. Although the professional game tends towards a 50:50 running:passing game, the colleges and high schools, as well as most British teams, will run far more often than they will pass. All successful offenses have at least one top-class running back on their roster and preferably two.

The running back has to be an all-round athlete. He not only has to run, but to block, catch and even pass during a game. He needs determination and courage to keep going against a strong defense, when every carry could mean getting hurt. It is a tough position to play, but also the most satisfying.

Full backs are generally bigger and slower than half backs. They carry the ball on quick hitting plays, but probably spend most of their time blocking for the half backs. Half backs need great pace and good moves. They will run behind their blockers for as long as possible, and then speed off for an extra few yards. Probably the only thing you can be sure of as a running back is that you will get hit – and hit hard.

## Stance

Running backs usually start from the same three-point stance as their linemen. They are normally between four and five yards from the line of scrimmage. As with linemen, their stance must not tip the play to the defense, so it is important to practise the stance, even though it is not as critical to the actual performance of the back, as it is to the lineman.

When playing as the tail back in the I-formation, it is usual to start from a two-point (base) stance. When coming from so deep it is more important to be able to see the defense than to start low.

## Blocking

Although the running back is chosen for his ball carrying abilities, he will not get very far without being able to block. Most British teams use three backs, with two of them blocking for the third. When a team is airing the ball, they will probably require the backs to stay where they are and pass protect. So they will almost certainly spend more time blocking than carrying.

The blocks you will commonly use are the drive block and cut block. Normally you will be smaller than the man you have to block, so your technique has to be good, and your attitude even better. Blocking by running backs is ninety per cent determination. If you want to stop him, you will.

Use the drive block wherever possible. Increase to top speed and make sure you aim below his shoulder pads. Assume the base position just before the collision, then keep your head up and your feet moving.

The cut block should only be used if the drive block fails. If you do it too often, the rushing defenders will anticipate the cut and easily throw you off, using your own momentum against you. You should also check your league's rules about the cut block, as some codes will only allow it near the line. If it is allowed, it can be useful when pass blocking. The back's job on a pass is usually to pick up any blitzing linebackers and the cut block may be the only way to stop them, especially if you spot them late. One tip when pass blocking – never move backwards. Chop your feet and as soon as anybody breaks into the pocket, move *forwards* to him. You must keep him from your quarterback.

## The Hand-Off *(Figs 29 & 30)*

The most common way to receive the football is by a hand-off (do not confuse this with the rugby 'stiff-arm'). I always tell players that the hand-off is the responsibility of the quarterback, and indeed it is, but that doesn't mean you should not make it easy for him. As the quarterback is going to give you the football, there is no need to look at it. Keep your eyes firmly on the hole and the defenders around it. The arm nearest the quarterback should be raised across your body and parallel to the ground. The outside arm should be under the ball with the elbow slightly out. Your arms should form a pocket for the football.

When you feel the ball in your stomach, close your arms around it and place your fingers over the ends. If you are running up the middle you should keep it hidden like this until you are clear of trouble. Do not grab at the ball. This means you are not looking where you are going, and you are also more likely to fumble the football.

Once you have control of the ball, and you are in no danger of an immediate hit, tuck the ball away under your outside arm. Keep your fingers over the end and squeeze it in tight. This will free your inside arm to help you run, and also to stiff-arm any opponent who comes too close. To change the ball from one arm to the other, put your free hand over the free end of the ball. Pass the ball across your body, still with both hands on it, and tuck it under the other arm. Only when it is secure should you release the two-handed grip.

Quarterbacks and running backs should practise hand-offs regularly. A fumble in the

Fig 29  Receiving a hand-off – notice the position of the back's arms.

Fig 30  Tuck the ball away.

backfield can be disastrous to the offense so repeat hand-off drills as often as possible.

## The Pitch Out

If you are running a wide play (sweep), you will lose valuable time if you have to wait for a hand-off. You want the ball as quickly as possible so that you can read the defense early and make your cut up-field. To achieve this, the quarterback will pitch the ball out to you. This is very similar to the rugby pass and the rules for receiving it are the same.

Keep your eye on the ball until you have it under control. For obvious reasons, this is opposite to the technique for a hand-off where you should keep looking at the hole. You should not meet a defender until well after

you have caught the ball, so practise running your route so that you can do it by instinct, and can watch the ball as it comes to you. Once you have caught the ball, tuck it away under your outside arm and look to head up-field.

## Faking *(Fig 31)*

Faking is as important as any other part of the running back's functions. You have to convince the defense that you have the ball while your team-mate blasts off in the other direction with it. The main thing about faking is to be conscientious. Any defender can easily spot the fake if you go at the line at half-pace, and stop running as soon as the quarterback has faked the hand-off. You must blast into the line, make a good show of getting the ball, and keep powering for at least five yards.

*Fig 31    When faking a run, you must convince the defense that you have the ball.*

# Running with the Ball
## *(Figs 32 & 33)*

Although running with the ball is an instinctive ability, anybody can improve their performance by developing a few basic techniques. The most common fault in runners is an inability to follow their blockers. This is a hangover from rugby and soccer where you are always taught to look for space, and then head towards it. If your coach has designed a play which gives you a lead blocker or two, keep close to them. Stay no more than one yard behind him, watching the closing defenders 'through' your blockers.

The stiff-arm technique is the same as the rugby football 'hand-off'. Extend your free arm towards the defender with your palm open and deliver a blow on his forehead or the top of

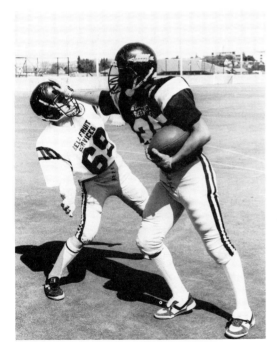

*Fig 32   The football 'stiff-arm' is similar to the rugby 'hand-off'.*

his helmet. It is important to hit him hard. Then lock your arm out and push off away from him. Practise this with both hands. Ideally, you should use a player holding a tackle dummy, or you can use a defender who is in the base position. (But change your partner regularly as he will get fed up with being hit so often!)

You should only use the stiff-arm if you have no alternative. Ideally, you do not want any form of contact at all. Techniques developed whilst playing rugby and soccer are quite appropriate here. A sudden change of pace will open up a space, as will the stutter step. This is stopping in full flight and then powering off again. That sudden stop will freeze the defender just long enough for you to get past. You can also use the side-step – run straight towards the defender and at the last moment take a sideways step with one foot. Then push off forwards. He will possibly get a hand on you, but your momentum will take you past him.

Always remember that your job is to make yards. Great lateral runs across the field may look impressive but will only serve to exhaust you. At the end of a run, all the previous techniques may be of no use to you. You have no blockers to help you and it is too tight to jink about. In these situations there is only one thing to do – be your own blocker. Wrap the ball up well in both arms, take up the base position (keep your head up) and drive into the defender. There is no real skill needed for this, just the desire hold out and grab any extra inches you can. As virtually all carries will end like this it is advisable to be ready for it.

In the section on sprinting, we mentioned that you should have a slight forward lean on your body. As a running back about to hit the line you should take this one stage further. Stay low, keeping your weight out in front of you. All the defender should see is your helmet, your shoulder pads and your knees. If you do this correctly and quickly, you will find

*Fig 33  Lean forwards and wrap the ball up just before you are hit.*

tacklers bouncing off you. However, don't assume you're tackled until you're down. Far too often I see players fall over at the first contact. Keep driving, even if you are stopped. Your second effort may gain a valuable yard, and every so often you will open up a big play.

## THE QUARTERBACK

Considering the quarterback is the linchpin of the offense, it may seem strange to put him at the end of this section on offensive techniques. I would recommend, however, that you do not play quarterback until you have a knowledge and understanding of all the other offensive positions. Concentrate especially on the running back techniques. If you have running ability your coach may design plays for you to carry the ball. There's also the possibility of a broken play, a missed hand-off that leaves you holding the ball, when you will have no alternative but to run.

On running plays the quarterback's job is as important as it is on a passing play, if not as glamorous. He must transfer the ball from the center to the running back. Any error will almost certainly mean a loss of yards and nothing lifts the defense more than a fumbled snap. It means they've got you worried. Probably the best piece of advice I can give to a quarterback is to know exactly what you have to do. When you leave the huddle you should know the snap count, the play, the point of exchange where you hand-off to the back,

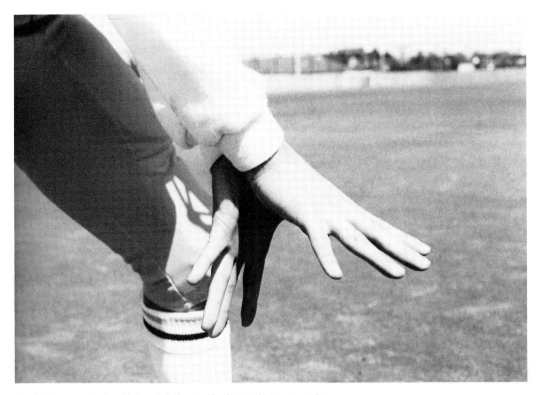

*Fig 34    The quarterback's hands in the position he would use to receive a snap.*

and also how you are going to get to that point.

Above all, stay calm. You are in charge out on the field and the rest of the team will look to you for leadership.

## The Snap *(Figs 34 & 35)*

As every play begins with the snap, you should practise it regularly so that it becomes a natural action. Place your hands so that the thumbs are parallel and touching. Your right hand (if you are right-handed), should be on top and the other hand to the left. Place your hands right into the center's crotch. (Don't be embarrassed!) He must be able to feel your hand, so apply a bit of pressure. This will also

make sure your hand moves forwards if the center moves forwards. Always maintain this hand contact until you have the ball.

Your feet should be shoulder-width apart and facing straight forwards. In fact, I recommend a slightly pigeon-toed stance. This will give you more stability, and also allow you to open out to a greater angle. Bend your knees slightly, keep your back straight and your head up. Look at the defense, not the center. When the ball is snapped, grasp it clearly and then pull it towards your stomach where you can protect it.

Step towards the point of exchange with the nearest foot. If you use a pigeon-toed stance you will be able to open out further. Take up the base position and, keeping the

Fig 35    *Immediately after the snap, pull the ball towards your stomach.*

ball in your stomach, move towards the point of exchange.

## The Hand-Off *(Fig 36)*

Remember that the hand-off is not the responsibility of the running back. It is up to you, the quarterback, to get the ball to him and let him worry about gaining yards. As you head towards the runner, stare hard at his stomach so that you can place the ball firmly into the pocket. (Be careful – too much force may wind him.) If you are a bit slow to the exchange, don't stretch towards him and fumble. Keep the ball yourself and, if you can, tuck in behind the back who will then become your lead blocker. At worst you will lose a few yards which is significantly better than a turn-over.

When you have to fake a hand-off, remember it has to fool the defense. So make everything look realistic. Look at the runner's stomach and put the ball there, but don't let go. Ride the ball forwards with him and then pull it away and hide it behind your hip. Keep your eyes on the back as he goes through the hole. If you look away immediately, your eyes will lead the defense to the real ball carrier.

## The Pitch-Out *(Figs 37 & 38)*

There are several ways to pitch-out the football, so I will show you the one I use. As the pitch-out is used on a wide play, it is quite common for a pulling guard to cross your face. It is important to give him room, so your first step must be backwards.

*Fig 36  This quarterback hides the ball with his body while faking a hand-off with his right hand.*

*Fig 37  To pitch out, first pull the ball on to your hip and step back with your far foot.*

Take the snap cleanly but do not pull the ball towards your stomach. Instead, put it against your right hip (if you are pitching to the left), and step back with your right foot. Next, step back with your left foot and open out towards the runner. Use the momentum of your turn to aid the pitch-out. Fix your eyes on the running back's numbers and aim for the ball to arrive about eighteen inches in front of him. Although rugby players normally spin the ball, I would not recommend this as it can make the smaller and harder American football more difficult to catch. If you can throw it without spinning, it will hang in front of the runner, just waiting to be caught.

## The Forward Pass
*(Figs 39 & 40)*

Passing a football is a bit like bowling in cricket. It is a matter of correct grip, good technique and spot-on timing. If you can pass the ball well, your team will be able to play to its full potential. If the defense know you are unlikely to complete a pass, they can move closer to the line and shut you down completely.

A good grip is essential to passing. The ball should be held firmly over the laces, with most of the pressure on your ring and little fingers. Spread your fingers wide and move your thumb round the ball so that it is opposite your middle finger. Most importantly, feel comfort-

able. The ball should be an extension of your hand.

Hold the ball in both hands, high on the right of your chest (if you are right-handed). Step towards your target with your left foot, looking over your left shoulder. Move the football up to your right ear. Whip your body round, square on to your target by pulling your left elbow down. Release the ball high (similar to a javelin throw). Keep the body turning and follow through with your right arm, stepping up with your right foot. If you put all your effort into the pass, your body should move through at least 180 degrees. Sometimes the force of the turn will cause you to fall over, but don't worry about it. Just make sure you get the ball away properly. If you do this correctly, you will find the spiral on the ball will come automatically.

Fig 38   Step back with your near foot, open out and pitch.

Fig 39   Spread your fingers to get a good grip of the ball.

(a)     (b)     (c)

*Fig 40   (a)   Hold the ball on your chest.   (b)   Step towards the target.*
*(c)   Turn, release and follow through.*

## The Drop

Although you will sometimes have to throw on the run, it is often much better to move back from the line and set yourself up for the throw. The drop is the name given to the three, five or seven steps that you take before you stop and throw. The three-step drop is used for short bullet passes, the five-step for mid-range throws and the seven-step for the spectacular bomb.

After taking the snap you should go to your passing position as quickly as possible. You know where your receivers are going, and your offensive line will take care of the defenders, so sprint your drop as fast as you can. Your first step (with your right foot if you are right-handed), should be a long one. As you

step, turn your body so that it is parallel to the sideline. Your second step should complete the turn so that your back is towards the line of scrimmage. Run through the remaining steps with your hips facing away from the line of scrimmage but with your upper body twisted so you can see down-field. When you stop, keep your feet chopping until you have seen your target, and then throw.

Practise your drops and passes with another quarterback, throwing the ball to each other. Adjust the angle and distance between you, to give a variation in the passes you have to throw. Two other drills you can use are to throw to another quarterback, but from a kneeling position (this develops arm power), and to throw to yourself whilst lying on your back (this improves technique).

# 3 Defensive Techniques

## BASIC DEFENSE

Defensive techniques can be split across the three sections of the unit – the defensive line, the linebackers and the secondary. Each of these sections will be discussed separately, but first we will look at those techniques that apply to all defenders.

## Tackling *(Figs 41 & 42)*

Quite simply, defense *is* tackling. If you cannot tackle, then do not play defense.

One of the great problems with coaching tackling in Britain is re-educating players from Rugby Union football. If you play rugby, you are taught to tackle low, with your head be-

Fig 41    A tackle from the front; get underneath him and hold on.

*Fig 42   Tackling from the side you must get your head in front of the runner.*

hind the runner. In American football, you must tackle high, with your head in front of him. In Rugby Union, it is usually sufficient to ground the ball carrier. The rules force him to release the ball and you can gain possession. In American football, not only must you ground him, but you must stop his advance. If you tackle him round the legs, his momentum will keep him going and he will gain a couple of yards simply by falling over. With only ten yards for a first down, you must not allow any yardage that you can prevent.

Even so, the golden rule is *stop him*. Tackling is 90 per cent determination and only 10 per cent skill, so even if you ignore all you are taught but can still keep knocking people over, you will have a place in the defense.

As you move in for the kill, keep your eyes on his belt buckle. There are two reasons for this:

1.   This is where you will hit him.
2.   He cannot fake with his belt buckle. His body will go where his belt buckle goes.

Just before contact, move into the base position (keep your head up!). Drive your shoulder into his stomach. If he is running across you, get your head in front of him. Tackling rugby-style, with your head behind, may allow him to break free. Once you have hit him, wrap your arms round and grab hold. Keep moving your legs and drive him back. Never let him drive you. If you can hit him upwards (as in a drive block), then all the better. If you lift his feet off the ground he cannot go anywhere, except where *you* want to take him.

You should practise tackling regularly. Ideally, the person being tackled should carry a tackle shield, but it is not essential. Tackle at walking pace, and simply lift the runner on to your shoulder. This will give you the correct technique. Also practise tackling from the side. After a few half-paced hits, try it at full speed.

Another tip is to keep your eyes open. Although you cannot help closing them at the moment of impact, it is surprising how many people close them a couple of paces before the hit. If you do, you cannot see if the runner side-steps or changes direction.

## Stripping the Ball *(Fig 43)*

Although the defense will have done its job by stopping the offense and forcing a punt, they can assist their own offense even more by gaining possession of the ball before the punt. The art of relieving the runner of the ball is known as *stripping*.

How you actually do this is up to you. You can pull, push, knock or punch the ball as long as you break it free. The important thing to remember is that your main job is to *tackle* the player. Don't go screaming in for man *and*

Fig 43   Gang tackling – the first defender has stopped the ball carrier, the second man attempts to strip the ball.

ball, and end up with nothing. The safest way is for the first player to the runner to tackle him. Once he is stopped, any other defenders arriving on the scene can attempt to strip the ball.

If you succeed in freeing the ball, make sure you recover it. Your first priority is possession – don't fumble the ball for the sake of advancing a few yards.

## Keys

The offense has two advantages over the defense: they know when they will snap the ball, and they know what the play is. What the defense has to do is minimise these advantages to such a degree that they become non-existent. To do this, watch the ball and/or certain players, and react to their movement.

This is known as *keying* and the player you watch is your *key*.

The respective keys for each position are given later in this chapter. Watch the offense at every opportunity, and notice how they line up. Is one of the running backs a bit edgy? Perhaps it's his turn to carry the ball. Do the receivers run out from the middle quicker than usual? This time it's a pass. Good defense depends on accurate reading of keys, so practise reading them from the very beginning.

## DEFENSIVE LINEMEN

Young linemen always prefer to play defense rather than offense, and the reason is simple. On defense, you will be given credit for your work. You gain marks for making tackles, and

Fig 44    *Defensive linemen can use the four-point stance as their initial action is a forward charge.*

a sack of the quarterback is often regarded as the highlight of defensive play. There is also the idea that the tactics of defensive line play are pretty basic and it doesn't take much to play there. As this section will show, it takes a lot of thought to play defensive line.

The defensive linemen must prevent the offense dominating the line of scrimmage on an inside run. They must be capable of mounting a good rush on the quarterback if the play is a pass. They must also have speed to move outside if a wide run develops.

## Stance *(Fig 44)*

Defensive linemen often use the same three-point stance as their offensive counterparts. It is quite suitable and allows good movement in all directions. Some coaches, however, prefer their defensive linemen to use a four-point stance. This is because their initial action is to charge straight ahead. As they do not have to pull left or right, they can put more weight on their hands. This will enable them to put more power into the forward surge, and also keep them lower than their opponent.

Take up the base position and drop your strongest foot back a few inches. Lean forwards and place both hands on the floor, directly under your shoulders. Keep your head up and your back parallel to the floor. This is the four-point stance. Another way to move into the stance is to drop on to your knees, place your hands on the floor and then push up on to your feet.

Fig 45    *The jam – get control of the blocker and then shed him to one side.*

## The Jam *(Fig 45)*

Most defensive coaches ask their linemen to destroy the offense's control of the line of scrimmage. The offense's knowledge of the snap count allows them a fraction of a second advantage, and if they use this to dominate the line of scrimmage it will be easy for them to move the football. They can merely run the ball behind their advancing lineman and grab four or five yards each play. As a defensive lineman you must prevent this happening. You cannot allow the offensive linemen to drive you off the line. Either you must drive them back yourself or remove them from the line altogether.

To knock them back requires hard work and good technique. Drive your shoulder in under your opponent's shoulder pads and bring your forearm up hard. Stop his charge by standing him up and then keep driving forwards. If you do this well, you can force a

center back into his quarterback or a tackle into a running back.

To remove them from the line we use the jam and the shed. Fire low out of your stance. Hit him upwards under the shoulder pads with your hands to stop his charge and stand him up. Extend your arms to full length and lock them out. Grab hold of his pads or his shirt – if you can keep hold of him, and keep him at arm's length, then you can dominate him.

## The Shed

Once you have a jam on your opponent, don't forget your assignment. Look for the football! Too often I see a defensive lineman so intent on dumping his opponent that he doesn't see the ball carrier running past. The offensive lineman's job is to move you away from the ball carrier, so you can bet that if he tries to move you to your left, the play is going to your right. Set up a good jam on him, feel which way he is trying to move you, and fight against it. Then lock your arms out and throw him out of the way. If he tries to move you left, shed him to your left and the ball carrier will run straight into you. This is called 'fighting pressure'.

## Pass Rush

If the play is a pass, the defensive lineman has one objective: to stop the quarterback from advancing the ball. The offensive lineman will not attack you, as on a run, but will retreat slowly, trying to keep you at arm's length by repeated stiff-arm hits. He will attempt to protect the quarterback and give him time to pass

to one of his receivers. If the defensive line can mount an effective rush, it will release the linebackers to cover the receivers.

A good pass rush is the most effective way to shut down a passing offense. The Chicago Bears, Superbowl Champions 1986, blitz linemen and linebackers all the time. Couple that with a good secondary and you will see why it is so difficult to pass successfully.

## Swim Technique *(Figs 46 & 47)*

This is a common way to beat a pass-protecting offensive lineman. Push at him and grab hold of the top of his shoulder pads. Push him back and his reaction will be to come at you. As soon as he does, twist him by

*Fig 46   The swim – grab the blocker and twist him.*

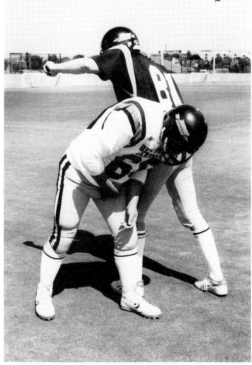

*Fig 47   Step with your inside foot and swim past him.*

pulling down and forwards with your right hand. Step by him, placing your left foot past his left foot. Then swing your left arm up and over his head (this is the 'swim'). As you bring it down, jam your elbow into his back and knock him away. Practise this until it becomes one smooth action. You must always maintain your forward momentum – if you stop running whilst you attempt the swim, you will end up dancing with him, and he'll be quite happy to do that all day.

As with run defense, don't forget what your assignment is. Keep your eyes on the quarterback. If you reach him before he passes, hit him high. Wrap your arms round him and knock him over. With luck you'll knock the ball free and a team-mate will recover it. If you can't reach him in time to stop him passing, you can still do some damage by putting your hands high in the air. If all the rushers do this, it causes a lot of problems for the passer and you will often manage to intercept the ball.

## Keys

The first thing you should key is the ball. Keep your eyes on it until the center snaps and then charge at your opponent. Remember that it is illegal to make contact with the offense before the snap, or to be in, or across, the neutral zone at the time of the snap. So key the ball, and don't move until it is snapped.

Your next key is your opposite number. Read from his actions what the play is, and then react. These are some general rules:

1. If he comes straight at you, fight the pressure.
2. If he pulls left or right, hold your ground. The temptation to run through the gap must be resisted. It is almost certain that another blocker has been assigned to you, so keep your eyes open. Scrape the line in the direction he pulled and fight through any blocks.

3. If he drops back, it is a pass, so rush the quarterback hard.
4. Be prepared to forget the first three rules! The offense will know how you read your keys so they may act to deceive you. They may drop back as if passing and then run (the draw play). Or they may fire at you and then pass (play action).

As you become more experienced, you will be able to take in more than just your own key. Using your peripheral vision you can view quite a large section of the offense, and their combined actions will tell you what you want to know.

## LINEBACKERS

Linebackers are the jacks of all trades on the defense. On one down they will be playing close to the line of scrimmage to stop the run, and on the next they will be dropping deep on pass defense. The play after that, they may be asked to rush the quarterback. The linebacker unit is usually subdivided into two parts – the middle (or inside) backers and the outside backers. They use the same techniques but have different responsibilities. One of the middle backers is usually the defensive captain. The coach may send in the basic instructions, but it is the defensive captain who is out there and he will be expected to adjust his coach's calls to suit the offensive alignment.

Most of the stops on the defense are made by the linebackers, so your tackling techniques should be flawless. You should be able to tackle from the front, the side and the rear. You also have to be intelligent. It is so easy to be lured out of position by a fake or 'misdirection'. Linebackers must assess the situation quickly and react instantly. Speed and agility are essential.

## Stance *(Figs 48 & 49)*

Linebackers use the two-point stance. Middle linebackers should be square-on, in the hitting position. On the snap of the ball they should take one pace forwards with their outside foot whilst they read the play. This will give them some momentum and ensure they are not caught flat-footed. Outside linebackers assume the hitting position and then drop the outside foot back. An important function of the outside linebacker is outside containment, and a staggered stance will enable him to carry this out effectively.

## Keys

Keys for linebackers will vary from team to team, and formation to formation. Your coach will tell you which players to key. Often you will have two keys, a lineman and a back. If this is the case, look at the back *through* the lineman. React to the lineman but keep your eyes on the back. In general, read the lineman, the same way as your own lineman would, that is, if he fires at you, it's a run, if he backs off, it's a pass. Again you should watch out for the draw or play action. Another play you should watch for is the screen. This is a play the offense uses against over-zealous linebackers, but it is easy to stop as long as you are alert. You must work on your keys and your reaction. If you take too long deciding what is happening, the play will be past you.

Fig 48    The middle linebacker should start in the basic two-point stance.

Fig 49    The outside linebacker is upright with his outside foot back.

# Defensive Techniques

## Meeting Blockers

If you are to tackle the ball carrier you will have to meet and remove his blockers. Having said that, you should never take on a blocker if you can possibly avoid it. Run past him and make that tackle. If you have to meet him use the jam and shed technique that we discussed earlier. As you move in on him, take up the base position and hit upwards with your hands through his shoulder pads. Use your legs to give more power to the jam. Knock him back on his heels, grab hold and then shed him. Don't waste time wrestling with him, get rid of him, and attack the ball carrier.

Instead of using the jam, you could also try to hit the blocker before he hits you. Use the drive block technique of putting your shoulder into his stomach and driving upwards. This will stop his charge and then you can run right past him. Meeting and removing blockers is a skill often neglected by inexperienced players but it is crucial to linebacker play.

## Scraping the Line

If the play is a run to your side (rather than straight at you), you are required to 'scrape' along the line to meet the carrier at the line of scrimmage. Don't charge straight into the backfield, as any decent running back will simply out-pace you. Instead shuffle along the line until you and the back collide.

To shuffle to the right, move your right foot out and then move your left foot up to it. This way you remain in the hitting position and stay square on to the line, so if anybody tries to block you, you are ready to join them. Shuffling is not as quick as running, but it is important not to cross your legs as you scrape the line. If somebody hits you when your legs are crossed you will go down like a ninepin. When you have finished scraping then you can turn and run.

## Outside Containment
### (Figs 50 & 51)

Imagine you are playing outside linebacker. You see the play develop as a sweep to your side. The initial reaction would be to charge straight in and make your tackle deep in the backfield. This is a good move, if it is successful; if it isn't, the running back will head for the sideline, cut down-field and break away for a big gain or touchdown. Instead, it is better to play the percentages. Your job as outside backer will probably be outside containment. (Sometimes your coach may give this assignment to another player.) Scrape along the line of scrimmage, maintaining a position just to the outside of the ball carrier. You are trying to force him to cut inside you. Your middle backers will also be scraping across and he will run into them. If he doesn't cut inside he will run straight into you or run out over the sideline. When you are experienced at this, you should move into the backfield whilst still maintaining that outside position. If blockers come to you,

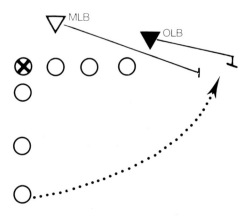

Fig 50   Outside linebacker contains outside and forces running back into middle linebacker.

*Fig 51    The outside linebacker (number 8) is maintaining an outside position on the runner to force him inside towards the scraping middle linebacker.*

meet them with your inside shoulder and throw them inwards. Whatever you do, make sure the back must cut inside you. Then, even if you miss your tackle, your team-mates will be able to stop him.

## Pass Defense

Your coach will give you an assignment to carry out every time you read pass. There are three main assignments you could be given: blitz, zone or man-to-man.

### Blitz

This is the fun part of linebacker play. You have just one aim – to sack the quarterback. Go in as fast as you can and pull, push, grab, claw, crawl, or whatever, to make sure you break through. By blitzing, you are reducing

your down-field coverage so you must succeed in your task. The phrase to remember is 'he who hesitates is lost'.

One word of caution: if you are playing outside linebacker and are told to blitz, be wary of the running back who moves out towards the sideline. He is moving out for a screen pass, so you must halt your charge and cover him man-to-man to prevent the completion. When blitzing, never let an opponent cross your face.

### Zone Defense (Fig 52)

Here, each player is given an area of field to cover. As a linebacker you will probably be allocated a zone about seven or eight yards from where you line up. As soon as you read pass, turn and sprint into your zone, keeping your upper body and head twisted back so

# Defensive Techniques

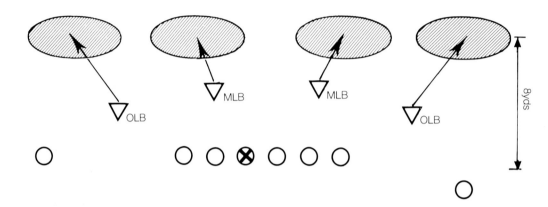

Fig 52   Basic linebacker zones.

you can see the quarterback. Watch for a possible draw or screen play. When you are absolutely convinced it will be a pass, look around for a receiver in your zone.

If a receiver moves deep through your zone, let him go. Your team-mates in the secondary will pick him up. If nobody enters your zone, look around at the other adjacent zones. One of your team-mates may have two receivers in his zone, if so go and help him out. If two receivers come into your zone, call for help and mark the one furthest from any potential help. When in a zone defense, you should always talk with other members of the defense. If you let everybody know you are in trouble, someone will come and help you.

## Man-to-Man

If you are asked to play man-to-man pass defense you will more than likely be told to cover the tight end or a back. Linebackers are not usually asked to cover fleet-footed wide receivers. The best way to play man-to-man coverage is to prevent the receiver actually running his pattern. If you can hold him up at

the line of scrimmage, you won't be caught out by a race down-field. Move right up to him and jam him or shoulder block him to the outside. Don't let him break inside and give the quarterback an easy pass. Make life as difficult as possible for the offense.

Once the ball is airborne, your job is the same whether playing zone or man-to-man. Firstly, you cannot make any contact with a receiver unless it is incidental whilst you are trying to catch the ball. Secondly, wherever you are, head towards the ball. Once it is in the air, you have as much right to it as the offense so fight for that football. Your first aim is to catch it but if you can't do that, then bat it away. Should there be two or three of you against one receiver, try and tip the ball upwards rather than bat it down. One of your team-mates could then catch it.

If you do make an interception, tuck the ball away and head towards their endzone. Your team-mates will move in front of you and run interference, so pick up as many yards as you can.

# THE SECONDARY

In its early days, football was a single unit game. There was no substitution, so the same eleven men played both offense and defense. The offense consisted of seven down linemen, a quarterback and wing back who were a yard off the line, and a full back and tail back five yards deep. When they turned round on to defense they used a similar formation. Seven down linemen, two linebackers and two deeper backs. In those days you were not allowed to pass the football forward so it was totally a running game. The nine players up close were expected to stop the offense. If they failed, the deeper backs formed a secondary line of defense.

Nowadays the secondary usually consists of three or four players and their main function is to stop the pass, especially the long bomb. Once they have established that there will be no pass, they also have run responsibilities. The trouble is that most players in the secondary are chosen for their pass coverage abilities. Although they have great speed, they are not normally very big, yet against the run they have to tackle sixteen-stone running backs. Their tackling techniques must therefore be first class. If the back gets past them, it usually means a touchdown.

## Stance

Playing deep in the secondary, your stance is not as critical as it is in other positions. Nevertheless, you should always adopt the two-point stance prior to the snap. As a coach I feel that a sloppy stance is an indication of a sloppy player. If you take up the two-point stance, you will be ready for anything the offense can send your way.

## Back-Pedalling

Once the ball is snapped you have to cover the receivers as well as keeping an eye on the ball. You do this by back-pedalling. Move into the base position, sit down even further and lean well forwards. Then dig in with your feet and move backwards as quickly as possible.

You must practise this technique regularly. Back-pedalling is an unnatural action and only constant repetition will let you feel comfortable. Practise back-pedalling twenty yards at a time. Concentrate on technique first, and then build up your speed. By being able to back-pedal you will keep yourself between the receiver and the endzone for as long as possible. Eventually you will have to turn and sprint but the longer you can put that moment off, the better. Vary the finish of your twenty-yard back-pedal – sometimes turn and sprint, other times break left or right or sprint forwards.

## Man-to-Man

Although zone defenses are more prevalent these days, you will still have to play man-to-man at some time. Your coach may suggest it as an alternative to trick the offense, or you may blitz all your linebackers. You must stick man-to-man with a receiver who enters your zone. Also, zones become impractical when the offense is down inside your ten-yard line.

There are several ways to play man-to-man defense, and your coach will tell you which he wants you to use on a specific down. The safest way is to line up about seven yards off your man and just to the inside. As he fires off at you, start to back-pedal. If he takes an angle to your inside, veer across with him. If he cuts outside, he has the sideline to worry about, and if he cuts inside you will have a head start on him.

As with all pass coverage, you must not let

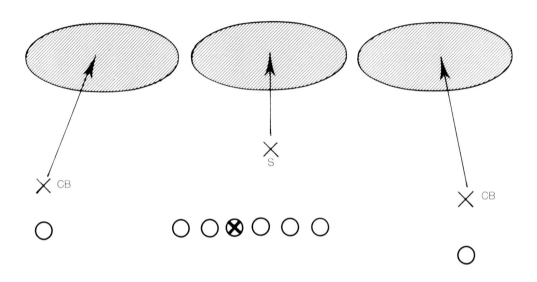

Fig 53   Deep zones are usually occupied by the defensive backs.

him get behind you. If you keep him in front, the worst that can happen is a completion – let him outrun you and he will score a touchdown.

The other common way of playing man-to-man is called 'bump and run'. If it works it is the best way of stopping a completion, but the risks are high. Line up almost right in front of the receiver, in a low hitting position. On the snap, uncoil upwards and really hit the receiver, trying to force him towards that sideline. Then turn and run with him. If you miss him, he'll be away, so your safety needs to be aware that you are playing bump and run, in order to keep an eye on you.

## Zone *(Fig 53)*

Playing in the secondary, you will normally be given deep zones to cover. Your drop is therefore similar to the linebackers' except that as you have further to drop, you must move

faster to get there. Turn and sprint back, but keep your eyes open, and watch the quarterback especially. Once you have reached your zone, set up in a good base position. Then pick up any player who enters your zone. If two people enter the zone, call for help. If nobody comes, look around to see if one of your team-mates needs assistance.

Invariably in a zone defense, there is a no man's land between the long and short zones. If a receiver moves into this area in front of your zone, think very carefully before moving to him. Only move when you are sure that a second receiver will not move into your zone as you vacate it.

## Aim for the Ball *(Fig 54)*

Once the ball is in the air it belongs to nobody. Make sure you head straight towards its landing site as fast as you can. Your first thought is an interception. For this you will need all the

*Fig 54    Once the ball is in the air, everybody should go for it.*

techniques of a receiver. If you can't intercept it yourself, then try and bat it away – if you can't have it, make sure he can't either. Finally, if you are sure you can't stop the completion, then make the tackle. If you can hit him as he collects the ball you can knock it free or at least stop any further gain. After one good hit on him, he will be listening for your footsteps rather than watching the football.

## Stopping the Run

Defensive backs should treat every play as a pass at its outset. Only when you are absolutely certain that it is a run should you leave your pass responsibilities and head for the ball carrier. One of the important skills of the secondary is the ability to make that decision as soon as possible.

To help make the decision you could watch the ball carrier. Once he crosses the line of scrimmage it is illegal for him to throw a forward pass. The trouble with this tactic is that you can be fooled by fakes and misdirections in the backfield. A better key is the guard and tackle combination on your side of the field. They are not allowed down-field on a pass, so if they move more than one yard forwards it must be a run. If they back off from the line it is almost certainly a pass.

One play which often catches out the inexperienced defensive back is known as the 'half back option pass'. The half back takes a hand-off or pitch out and runs wide as on a sweep. He hopes the secondary will read run and move in for the tackle, then he zips a pass out to his receiver who has been left wide open. Read the play quickly, but read it cor-

## Defensive Techniques

rectly. If you are in any doubt, treat it as a pass, then at least you won't let the opposition through for a big gain.

A final word about tackling: nobody is going to expect you to hit a sixteen-stone running back like a linebacker would. Just do anything you can to stop him. If you can't manage a good tackle, grab his shirt, or pants, or anything you can and hang on until help arrives. As long as you stop him scoring, you will have done your job.

# 4 Kicking Techniques

Football is not just offense and defense. On average, twenty to twenty-five per cent of all downs involve kicking the ball. You kick off at the beginning of each half and after a score. If you fail to make ten yards after three downs, you will almost certainly kick, either a field goal or a punt. After a touchdown you can claim an extra point if you kick the ball between the uprights.

Although these kicking units are known as *special teams*, they are basically extensions of the offense and defense. Kick-off teams are usually defensive, whilst punting and goal-kicking teams are part of the offense. On all these teams, the man who kicks the football is the key player. A long kick-off will peg the opposition back inside its own 20-yard line and give your defense more chance of success. If your offense's drive has halted, a good punt can motivate the whole team, and you must regularly kick field goals.

If you are a punter or a goal-kicker, you will rapidly discover that it is very lonely out there. Whilst you can do nothing except get your kick away, there are eleven defense players trying to make sure you don't. And if you do foul up, everybody will spot it. To be a kicker, you need a good nerve as well as good technique.

## Punting *(Fig 55)*

If you have played rugby, you will know how to punt the football. In fact, punting in American football took its name from the rugby punt.

You should stand twelve to fifteen yards behind the line of scrimmage. Hold your hands out in front of your body, ready to catch the ball. If the snap is a bit wayward, get your body behind the ball by shuffling left or right. Don't lean or stretch. Then step with your kicking foot, step with the other foot and kick. You must perfect this one-two-kick rhythm. If you take longer, your kick could well be charged down. After the kick, follow through so that your kicking foot is level with your hand.

With a punt, you need height as well as

Fig 55   *The punter must have a good follow-through.*

distance. A high kick will allow your team more time to get down-field. If you are not achieving both, the most likely cause is the transfer of the ball from your hand to your foot. A common fault is to throw the ball upwards. You should drop the ball on to your foot, and time the drop to coincide with the swing of your leg. The ball should hit your foot at an angle so that maximum contact is made. If you take hold of the ball with your thumb along the seam, and then hold it out with your fingers pointing forwards, the ball will be at the correct angle for punting.

When you practise punting, concentrate on style rather than strength. You will gain more height and distance with the correct technique than you will by just trying to kick it hard.

Fig 56   When kicking for goal, always keep your head down until you have finished your follow-through.

## Goal-Kicking *(Fig 56)*

There are two styles of goal-kicking. The straight-on (American) style or the soccer style (side-winder). For years the straight-on method alone was used, but the influx of Europeans into the States has led to an increase in the use of the side-winder.

In Britain, where everybody is brought up on soccer, virtually all goal-kickers use the side-winder method. It is far more accurate because a larger area of your foot makes contact with the ball. If you kick straight-on, contact is only made with your toe and the slightest error will send the ball off at an angle. By kicking soccer-style you do sacrifice some distance, but if you can consistently kick goals from within thirty-five yards, the odd miss from greater distances should not be so crucial.

Goal-kickers in Britain are usually allowed to use a two-inch block on which to place the ball. This gives more height to your kick and makes lifting the ball over a charging defense much easier. If your league rules allow it, I would recommend using the block.

As with punting, goal-kicking is more a question of technique than strength. Place the tee seven yards behind the ball. (For some unknown psychological reason it is easier to kick a goal if you put the block down yourself, rather than let your holder put it down!) Take three paces back and then two paces to the left (if kicking right-footed). Then use the one-two-kick rhythm again. The key to goal-kicking is the placing of the non-kicking foot. It should be pointing at the post and level with the block. Make sure you plant it firmly and then kick, following through as in the punt. You should make contact about two to three inches above the block. Keep your eye on the ball as you kick and don't lift your head until you have completed the follow-through.

If you are inaccurate, experiment with the placement of the non-kicking foot. Move it back to get more height, and forwards for more distance. If you are hooking the ball, move it sideways, away from the block; if slicing, move it nearer.

## Team-Mates

To punt and goal-kick successfully, you have to work in harmony with some of your team-mates, so practise punting with your center, and goal-kicks with your center and holder. All three of you must know each others' actions and timings well, to ensure maximum efficiency and success.

## Kick-Off

Kicking-off is the easiest kick to perform. The ball is placed on a special tee on your 35-yard line. Nobody is trying to hit you so you can take as long a run-up as you need. Remember, though, that it is the final speed of your foot which affects the kicks, not the speed of your body. So don't sprint to the line and then take a lazy swing at the ball. Use your run-up to maximise the final velocity of your leg.

With our soccer and rugby backgrounds, there are plenty of people with good technique in the British leagues, so the choice of kicker often comes down to a question of mental attitude. You need a cool head and nerves of steel. If you have to punt from your own endzone, or kick a field goal in the last seconds to win, then you can't be thinking of failure. Always think positively. Imagine your kick soaring away and you'll almost certainly succeed.

# 5   Offensive Game

## OFFENSIVE GAME PLAN

The offensive game plan will consist of plays and formations that you or your coach feel will work against the opposing defense. If you know your opponents well, you will devise special plays to use solely against them. In pro football, and the senior college leagues, teams prepare play books containing hundreds of plays for use in all situations. Ideally, players should be available to practise for several hours every day. In Britain, however, the average team can only practise two or three times a week. If this is the case, design about twelve plays to cover a range of circumstances – passes, inside runs, off-tackle runs, sweeps, and so on. Then practise these few plays until you can run them perfectly. Successful offense depends on consistently executing your plays. Concentrate on eradicating fumbles and mistakes. Do not give away penalties. Then hit your opponents hard and fast. Football can be a simple game and if you over-complicate it, you will only introduce more chances to make an error.

## Huddle

The down starts when you enter the huddle. The huddle is where you are informed by the quarterback what the next play will be. It can also be a useful place to exchange information. Perhaps your opponent is moving to the outside when you use a certain formation. Tell your quarterback and he will call a play to take advantage of the situation. It is *not* a place to criticise your team-mates. If you speak, it should only be to the quarterback, and then only speak if you have something useful to say.

The quarterback should be in control of the huddle. If he appears nervous or indecisive it will rub off on the rest of the team. He should speak clearly and firmly. The other players should look at the quarterback's mouth and listen carefully. The quarterback will call the play by calling the formation, the play and the snap count. He should repeat the information to make sure everybody understands the call. Then he says 'break', and the players leave the huddle, moving to their starting positions. Wide receivers should sprint from the huddle as they have further to go.

There are two basic types of huddle: open and closed.

### Closed Huddle (Fig 57)

The closed huddle is the type usually used by the pro teams seen on the television. Players always stand in the same position in the huddle. The center usually sets the huddle ten yards from the ball, and the other players form a circle round him with their hands on their knees. It is difficult for the opposition to see what is happening in the closed huddle and this makes it popular in the NFL.

### Open Huddle (Fig 58)

The open huddle is more common in college and high school football. Coaches prefer it because it cuts down talking by players other than the quarterback. Anybody causing a problem can be seen by the coach. In pro football the discipline is better so the open

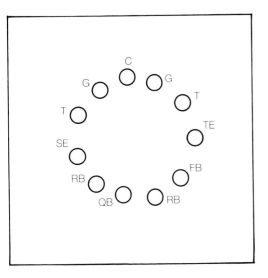

Fig 57    The closed huddle as used by pro teams.

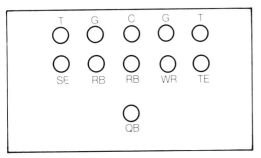

Fig 58    The open huddle is used by many college and high school teams so that the coach can keep his eye on his players between downs.

huddle is not needed. Its disadvantage is that the defense can see what is going on as well – they may notice two players talking to each other and gain a clue to the play.

The open huddle can be lined up so that all players (except the quarterback) can either face, or have their back to, the defense, depending on the coach's preference. Some like their team to keep their eyes on the opposi-

tion, whilst others prefer them to concentrate on the quarterback. The players at the back stand upright, whilst those in the front row put their hands on their knees.

## Play Calling

As stated earlier, the quarterback will call the formation, the play and the snap count. There are many ways to do this, and your coach will tell you your team's system, but this section explains a system in common use.

Formations are given a name such as the I, the pro, or the wishbone. These formations usually have a strong side and a weak side. The strong side is the one on which the tight end lines up – which can be either the left or the right side. You can call formations as 'I-left' or 'wishbone-right'.

Running plays are normally called by stating the ball carrier, the hole he is running through and the blocking assignments. The first two of these are usually identified by numbers, and the blocking by a name. A possible scheme for back numbering is shown in *Fig 59*, and a system for hole numbering in *Fig 60*.

Blocking assignments are given names like dive, blast, trap. Putting all these together you can call a play like '42-blast'. This would indicate that the half back (4) would run be-

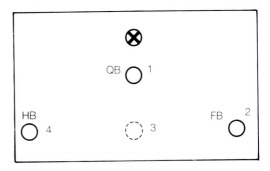

Fig 59    Numbering the backs.

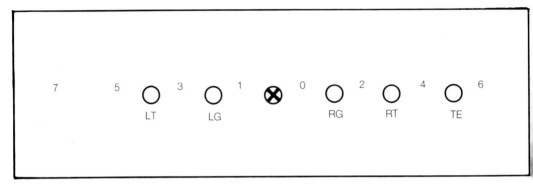

*Fig 60   Hole numbering. If the quarterback wants a run by the half back between left guard and tackle, he calls a 43 run.*

tween his right guard and tackle (2 hole) with blast blocking.

Snap counts are also many and varied. A good basic snap count is 'ready – down – set – hut'. Players get into their two-point base on 'ready'. On 'down' they move into their three-point stance. They can then go on 'set' or 'hut'. If you use motion, the motion man can move on 'set' and the team can go on 'hut'. You can also throw in a second or third 'hut'. Keep varying the snap count and you will stop the defense anticipating your moves.

The complete call from the quarterback will then sound something like this; 'I-right, 24-drive, on set'.

## Formations

The history of football is also the history of offensive formations. Teams develop an offense for their players and defenses change to counteract it. There is no 'best' formation, only the best formation for your team. Several years ago teams would use one formation alone, but nowadays it is common for teams to use several line-ups. This means there is more to learn and perfect, but it also means that defenses have to be more versatile to stop you.

Choose your formations to suit your team. If your players are big and slow, choose a formation that allows you to pound away inside. If they are small and fast, use a formation that allows you to move outside quickly (such as the T). If you have a great throwing quarterback, use a passing formation (such as the split). If your players are big *and* quick you can run whatever you want!

### The Split or Open Set (Fig 62)

This is a common formation used by the pros. It has two wide receivers and a tight end to catch passes. The backs are split out so that they can take their places in the pass pocket. You can run outside from this formation but middle runs are more difficult.

### The Pro Set (Fig 63)

This is similar to the split, in that it also has two wide receivers. By bringing one of the backs nearer the center, it improves the middle running on the strong side, but weakens it on the weak side.

Fig 61    John Elway audibles at the line.

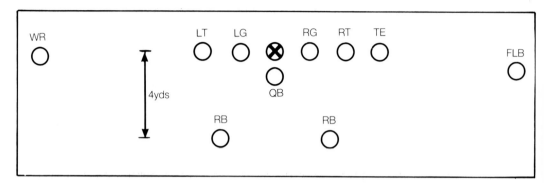

Fig 62    The split formation. This is particularly good for passing and running outside.

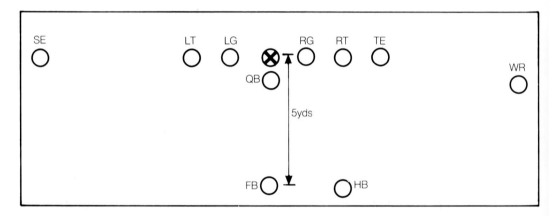

Fig 63    The pro-set.

## The Twin Set (Fig 64)

Another relation of the split set, the twin set has both wide receivers on the weak side. By standing only five or so yards apart, these two can co-ordinate their routes to confuse the defense.

## The I (Fig 65)

This is also a two-receiver formation which is stronger running up the middle, but at the expense of outside sweeps. The full back is five yards behind the center and the tail back is

two yards behind him. This pairing of backs can hit effectively either side of the center, with the full back blocking for the tail back. However, it is slow in developing outside as the backs have further to run.

## The Power-I (Fig 66)

The power-I was developed by John McKay of the University of Southern California during the 1960s. It has only one wide receiver, the second man being replaced by a third running back. This is primarily a running formation which still retains the option of the pass. It is

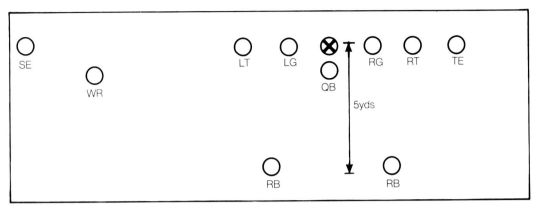

*Fig 64*    *The twin-set. The two wide receivers on one side can lead to interesting crossing routes.*

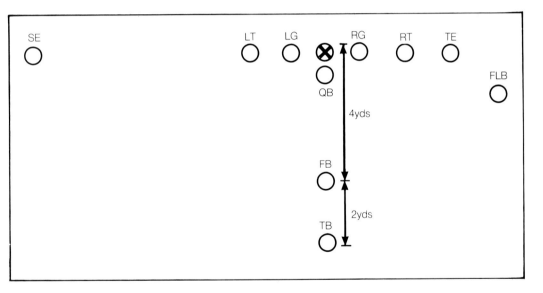

*Fig 65*    *The I-set. This is another strong passing formation that is also good for inside running.*

very strong running between the tackles, but is unbalanced, so that defenses may adjust to the position of the extra back. The key player is the tail back who will usually have two blockers in front of him.

## The T (Fig 67)

This is a strong running formation, often used without a split end. Two tight ends are used instead. It is balanced so that any of the three backs can hit along the line. It is difficult to run inside with blockers, but a sweep will enable

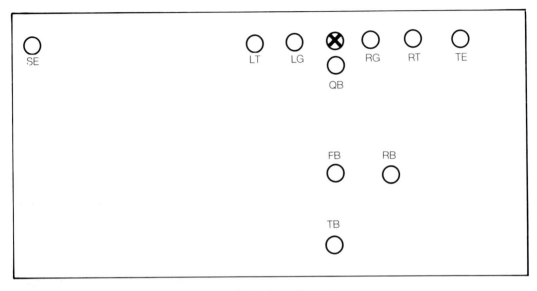

*Fig 66  The power-I. A variation of the I-set which is primarily used for inside running.*

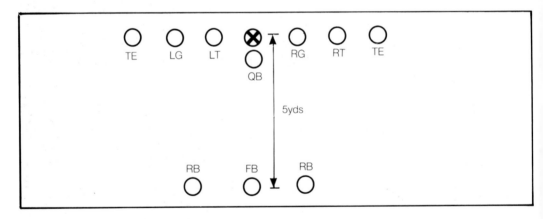

*Fig 67  The T.*

two backs to get out in front of the ball carrier.

## The Wishbone (Fig 68)

In the wishbone, the full back steps up-field a pace from the other two backs. This allows middle runs to have one or two blockers in front of the carrier. The wishbone has developed alongside one specific play – the triple option. This will be discussed later in this chapter.

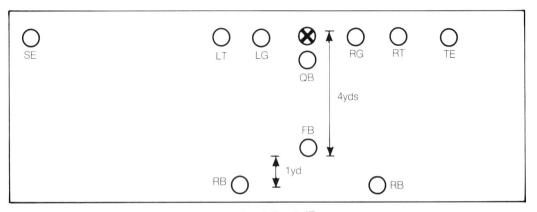

Fig 68    The wishbone formation was popularised by Darryle Royal of Texas
University during the 1960s.

Fig 69    Mike Tomczak behind the Chicago Bears' offensive line (American
Bowl 1986).

# THE RUNNING OFFENSE

There are only two ways to advance the football. You can run with it, or you can pass it. If you can do both well, you obviously keep the defense guessing. If they know that you never pass the ball, they will close up on the line. If you always pass, the defense can remove its linebackers and play with seven or eight men in the secondary. So you must work on both aspects of offense, even if you do not have a fifty:fifty split between running and passing. It is quite possible to use a ninety:ten split, as long as the alternative threat is there.

Running with the ball was originally the only way forwards. It may not be as spectacular as passing but it is effective and far less risky. All teams should have certain running plays in their armoury. They must have runs up the middle, off-tackle and round the outside. They must use misdirection, fakes and draws. Only when you can run these 'bread and butter' plays consistently should you start to develop more complex gimmick plays such as reverses and flea-flickers.

Only the more traditional runs are discussed here. The names of these plays are fairly standard although your coach may well call them something else.

## The Dive *(Fig 70)*

The dive is the most basic of all runs. The offensive line must power forwards and knock the defense back off the line of scrimmage. A single running back, without lead blockers, runs behind his line gaining as many yards as he can. The ball carrier is normally the bigger and stronger full back, although the ball can be given to any of the other backs. The example shown is from the split formation, but dives can be run well from any of the common sets – they will just hit at different places. The split formation will hit either at hole two or hole three. The pro will hit at hole zero or hole one if the full back carries, or hole two or hole three if the half back carries.

The important factor in the dive play is speed. Use a short snap count and hit the line as quickly as possible. The dive is usually only

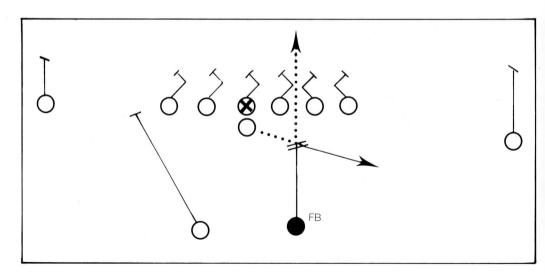

Fig 70   *The dive (split right, 22-dive).*

Fig 71   Eric Dickerson – the Rams' record-breaking running back.

a short yardage play but it can break for long gains. The quarterback should open out towards the hole and hand off firmly to his back.

This play works well against middle linebackers who are hanging deep anticipating a pass or a sweep.

## The Blast *(Fig 72)*

The blast is also a quick-hitting play. This time the ball carrier has one or two blockers in front of him. It is normally run with double team blocking by the line. This will leave a defender free, but the lead blockers are there to deal with him. The quarterback must get the ball to the tail back as quickly as possible, so he should turn and run back at an angle so he can make a deep hand-off. The tail back himself must stay behind his blockers. There is a tendency to see a mass of bodies in the hole and to run wide. However, if he tucks in behind his blockers, they will make a hole for him, although it will not appear until very late in the run.

The blast is effective against loose middle

backers when it can break for long yardage. It is also a good short yardage play.

## The Triple Option *(Fig 74)*

The wishbone formation goes hand in hand with the triple option. The quarterback has three choices after the snap: he can hand the ball to his full back; he can run the ball himself behind one of his half backs; or he can pitch the ball out to his other half back. There are plenty of high school and college teams who run this single play as virtually their total offense. It needs a strong, durable full back and a quick running quarterback. It is not seen in pro football as it puts too much strain on the quarterback. In amateur football, the quarterbacks are considered expendable.

The key to the triple option is the outside linebacker – whatever he does should be wrong. As soon as the quarterback receives the snap, he fixes his eyes on the outside backer. If the backer moves outside, the quarterback hands off to his full back. If the backer

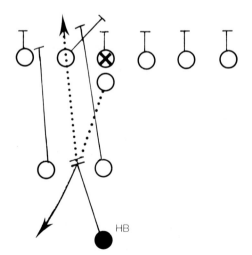

*Fig 72   The blast (power-I right, 43-blast).*

Fig 73    On a blast play, the quarterback must get the ball to the half back as deep as possible.

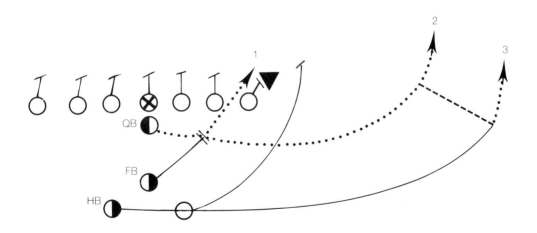

Fig 74    The triple option. After the snap the quarterback can either: make a hand-off to the full back (1); run the ball using a half back as a blocker (2); or pitch out to the other half back (3).

moves inside to stop the full back, the quarterback fakes the hand-off and carries the ball himself. His half back will be trailing him, about a yard behind and three or four yards outside. If the defense closes on him, he can pass laterally to the half back.

Another version of this play has the full back hitting between the guard and tackle. This time the quarterback will key the defensive tackle. On all versions of this play, if the full back does get the ball the remaining backs must continue running as if the quarterback had kept it. Keep the defense guessing who has the ball.

## The Sweep *(Fig 75)*

This is a wide play, with lead blocking and pulling guards. After you have forced the defense to overload the middle of the line by running dives and blasts, you then hit them with a sweep. The two guards must get out quickly and beat the ball carrier to the line. The far-side guard should trap anybody who comes through the hole left by the other guard,

otherwise he should keep going until the half back turns up-field and then cut up-field himself.

The quarterback pitches the ball out to the half back who should follow his full back and the run-side guard. They should move up-field and take on the defense once they are past the tight end. It is common for teams to head wide and wait for the hole to appear of its own accord. This, of course, does not happen, and the play merely moves laterally until the players run out across the sideline.

## The Counter *(Fig 76)*

The counter is an off-tackle play off a misdirection fake by the full back. The full back fakes a dive to hole one. The half back takes one step towards that hole and then cuts outside the quarterback and receives the hand-off. The far-side guard pulls and leads the half back through the off-tackle hole. As in all plays with lead blockers, the ball carrier should keep behind him for as long as possible – let your blockers do all the work.

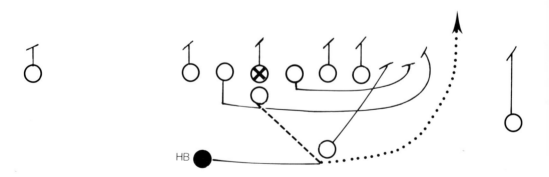

*Fig 75  The sweep (split right, 46-sweep).*

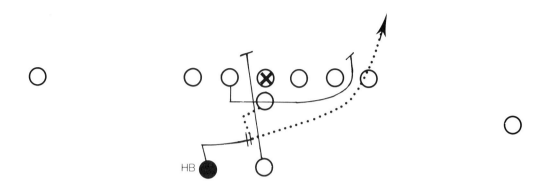

*Fig 76    The counter (pro-right, 44-counter).*

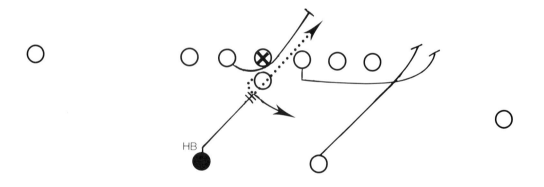

*Fig 77    The trap.*

This is a good play for keeping linebackers 'honest'. They will hesitate on dives and blasts if they get caught by the counter.

## The Trap *(Fig 77)*

A trap play is one where a defensive lineman or linebacker is not blocked on the line. The defender charges over the line of scrimmage hoping to make a big play when he is hit from the side by another blocker. There are many variations of the trap. The one shown here is designed to look like a sweep. As the linebacker follows the pulling right guard he is trap blocked by the left guard. The ball carrier then runs through the gap created by the trapped defender. It is an effective play against teams playing wide to stop the sweep, and a good fake pitch-out will assist in the illusion.

## The Draw *(Fig 78)*

When your team is running, your linemen will fire down-field to blast a hole. When you are passing, your linemen will drop back to pass protect. This makes it very easy for the defense to decide whether you are about to run or pass. The draw play is designed to upset the defense's quick thinking and cause them to delay for a second. The draw play is a run that looks like a pass.

At the snap, the linemen drop back to form their pocket. The receivers run deep patterns. The quarterback drops back three steps then hands off to the half back who blasts between center and guard with his full back leading. If the defense read pass, the linebackers will drop into their zones. The pass rushing linemen will be concentrating on getting to the quarterback. Once the ball carrier has crossed the line of scrimmage there should be an

area of six or seven yards without a defender in it.

This play is very effective against a hard pass rush. It can also cause linebackers to hesitate before dropping into their zones.

## The Reverse *(Fig 79)*

The reverse is just one of many gimmick plays used by football teams. The main advantage it has is surprise, so it will only work once in a game. Its disadvantage is that the ball is in the backfield for a very long time, so if it fails, you'll probably incur a large loss of yardage. Still, it is fun to do, and the crowds love it.

Basically it looks like a sweep, but after the half back catches the pitch out, he hands off to a wide receiver running in the opposite direction. This move works well if your quarterback can lead block for the receiver.

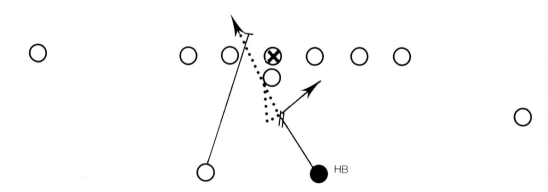

*Fig 78   The draw (split right, 41-draw).*

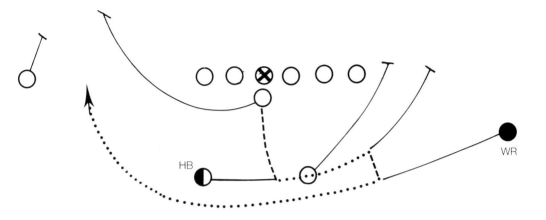

*Fig 79    The reverse (split right, 46-sweep, reverse left).*

# THE PASSING OFFENSE

Someone once said, 'There are three things that can happen when you pass, and two of them are bad'. The three things he was talking about are a successful catch, an incompletion and an interception. At NFL level he could well be right, but at lower levels of football we may take a slightly different view. A completed pass is obviously what we are after, and an interception is an unmitigated disaster, but an incomplete pass is rarely more than an inconvenience. Most teams in Britain use the pass to set up the run, and an incomplete pass does nearly as much to keep the defense honest as does a completed one. Far more serious is to have your quarterback sacked. This will invariably mean a loss of yards, and if he fumbles the ball, you are really in trouble.

When developing a passing offense, top priority must be given to protecting the quarterback. You must make every effort to enable him to pass the ball. This can mean keeping your backs and tight ends in the pocket and using two receivers, or possibly only one receiver. If you do use only one receiver, then you should call a route for him to run, but give him licence to alter that route as he reads the defense. His main aim must be to get open.

## The Drop Back Pass *(Fig 80)*

This is the classic pass run by most pro teams. The quarterback takes the snap and drops back three, five or seven paces. He then turns and throws. His linemen will retreat into a semi-circular shaped pocket to give him all-round protection. The backs will key the backers on each side and also help out the line if somebody penetrates.

The drop back pass offers maximum protection to the quarterback. Its disadvantage is that it is so obviously a pass that defenses will quickly marshall their pass coverages and make a completion harder to achieve.

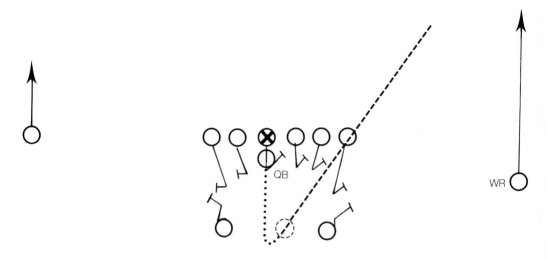

*Fig 80    The drop back pass.*

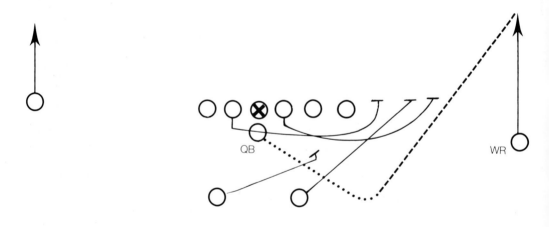

*Fig 81    Roll out pass.*

## The Roll Out Pass *(Fig 81)*

Here the quarterback runs back and out towards the sideline. He is usually protected by
his backs and by both his guards who pull
along the line of scrimmage. The quarterback
has the option to run on a roll out pass. He will

do this if the defense backs off to protect
against the pass. If they attack him, then he
will pass the ball. The quarterback should key
the defense whilst running this play and
should be moving towards the line of scrimmage before he passes. This achieves two
things: firstly the defense will think you are

Fig 82   To throw accurately on the run is a skill that does not come easily, but
         Joe Montana is one of the best.

running and move in for the tackle; secondly the momentum of your run will assist your pass.

Roll out passes are normally only run to one side of the field. Right-handed quarterbacks will roll out to the right and left-handed quarterbacks to the left. Only the very best quarterbacks are able to twist and throw accurately whilst running against their throwing arm.

## Play Action Pass *(Fig 83)*

The play action pass is the opposite of the draw play. It is a pass that is designed to look like a run. You should use your best running plays so that the defense is drawn in, and then fake the hand off. Drop back a yard or two, set up and throw. Your linemen must remember not to advance more than one yard across the line of scrimmage as this is illegal on a pass play. They must hold up their opponents without driving them back.

## The Screen *(Fig 84)*

The screen pass is a special version of the pass. The build up is as for a drop back or play action pass. Whilst this is going on, a running back has moved laterally out towards the sideline. The quarterback throws him the ball, and at the same time two or more linemen pull out and form a screen in front of him as he runs up-field.

This is an effective play when it works but it takes great timing by all concerned, so you must practise it often.

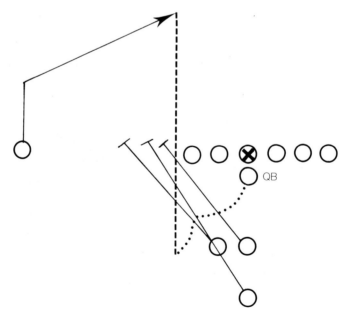

Fig 83   Play action pass.

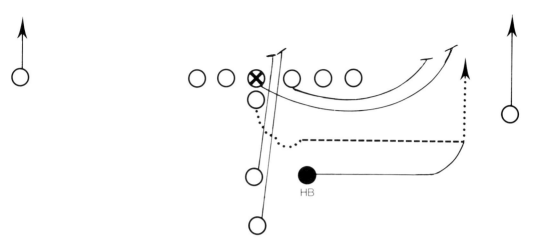

Fig 84    Screen pass (off play action fake).

Fig 85    New York Jets' quarterback Ken O'Brien rolls out to pass, holding the
ball securely in both hands.

# Offensive Game

## Patterns *(Figs 86 to 88)*

We have already discussed the individual routes which a receiver may run. The set of routes run by all the receivers is known as a pattern. Patterns are designed to do several things. Against man-to-man marking they make sure all the defenders are occupied and no receiver has double coverage. Against the zone they will be used to overload a defender by placing two or three receivers in the same area of the field or to pull the zone apart by drawing a defender out of his zone and sending someone in behind him (*Fig 86*).

Another way to beat the pass coverage is to send a running back out from the backfield. The wide receiver draws the defense away and the half back runs into the gap (*Fig 87*).

Timing patterns are designed for the three receivers to make their cuts one after the other. The quarterback looks towards the first. If he is not free he looks to the second, and finally to the third. In the pattern shown in *Fig 88* the quarterback's primary target is the flankerback running a 5-out. If he is covered, he looks to the tight end who is just breaking on his hook pattern. Finally, if these two are covered, the split end, who has run a slow developing zig-zag route, should be free.

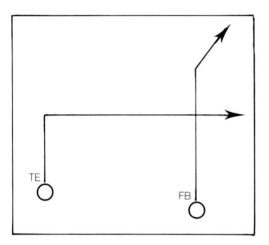

(a)

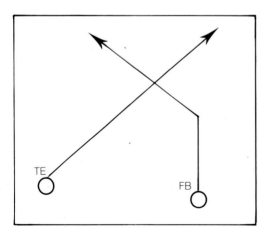

(b)

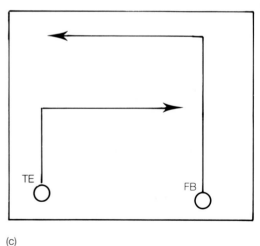

(c)

Fig 86   Some common patterns: (a) out-flag; (b) slant-post; (c) out-cross.

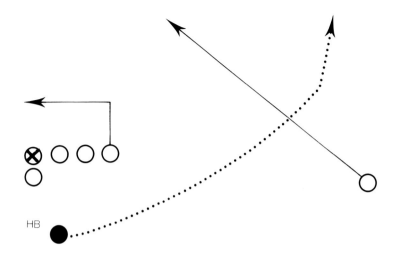

*Fig 87    Quite often the defense will miss a back coming out of the backfield.*

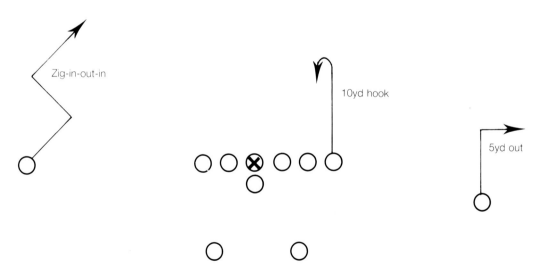

Zig-in-out-in

10yd hook

5yd out

*Fig 88    Example timing pattern.*

## Scrambling

No matter how many times you practise your passing plays, there will come a time when the offensive line will not hold and your quarter-back will be forced to scamper around, trying to avoid being sacked. This is called scrambling.

When this happens, the receivers should go into their scramble drill. They must forget their prescribed routes and drift back towards the line of scrimmage, but in the direction that the quarterback is scrambling. They must stop, start, twist and turn in order to get free and they must wave their arms. The quarterback will be occupied with avoiding the sack, so the receivers must make themselves as obvious to him as they can.

## The Half Back Option *(Fig 89)*

Although the majority of passes are thrown by the quarterback, other players are also allowed to pass the ball. The most common play to use this is the half back option pass. The play looks like a sweep and depends on the secondary over-reacting and closing in on the half back. If they do, he makes a bomb pass to his wide receiver. If they drop back for the pass, he runs for the easy yardage. It is important to remember that the pass must be thrown from behind the line of scrimmage and that the linemen must not advance more than

one yard over the same line until the pass has been made.

# OFFENSIVE SPECIAL TEAMS

There are three teams on offense that are considered 'special': the punting team, the goal-kicking team, and the kick-off return team.

## Punting Team *(Fig 90)*

The punting team is usually called on to the field when the offense is on fourth down and out of range of their field goal kicker. There are two phases to the job of the punting team. Firstly, they must get the kick away and secondly they must cover down-field to prevent the return.

Pro teams usually use a spread formation

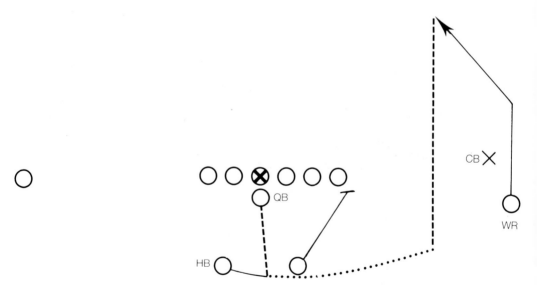

*Fig 89  The half back option pass. The half back keys the corner back. If he drops back, the half back will run; if he closes for the tackle, the half back passes.*

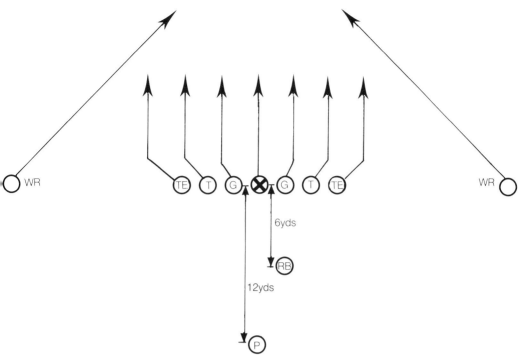

WR    TE   T   G   ⊗   G   T   TE    WR

6yds

RB

12yds

P

Fig 90    The punting team protects the punter and then moves down-field to
          stop the return.

Fig 91    Denver's John Elway shows his scrambling ability as he avoids the
          Jets' Joe Klecko.

with one-yard gaps between the linemen. Junior teams tend to use the tight-punt formation, in which the linemen set up with six inches between each other. The punter is twelve yards behind the center with a blocker six yards behind the right guard (if you have a right-footed punter). When the center snaps the ball, the two wide players sprint down-field heading straight for the returner. The center stands his ground and the other linemen block to their inside. Nobody should be allowed to penetrate the line – if they do, the blocker must pick them off. Once the ball is kicked, the linemen release their blocks and fan out down-field, the two tight ends containing the outside. The blocker and the punter trail the play, acting as the safeties.

If teams regularly return punts against you, it is usually because you don't move down-field quickly enough. Never follow a team-mate, but stay in your coverage lane – and don't miss your tackles. The punting team doesn't always punt the ball. There are other options available and it is as well to have them in your play book. Their big advantage is surprise and you should be able to pick up the one or two yards needed to gain the first down.

To run from the punt formation, the center snaps the ball to the blocker who dives through the line, with cross blocking by his linemen. If you pass from this formation, the ball is snapped to the punter as usual. He takes his first two steps as if he is going to punt but then rolls out to his right (or left) and fires the ball at his receiver.

## Goal-Kicking Team
### (Figs 92 & 93)

The goal-kicking team is used for field goal attempts and for the extra point after a touchdown. The techniques and tactics for these manoeuvres are identical except that for field

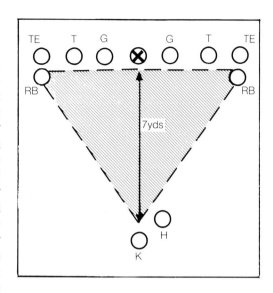

Fig 92   Goal-kicking team. The offense must not let any defenders into the triangle.

goal attempts teams must be prepared to stop a run back by the defense if the kick misses or is short.

The linemen set up with their feet touching. The two backs stand behind the ends, facing outwards, with their hands on their knees. These nine players must prevent anybody entering the seven-yard triangle.

It is possible to execute a passing play from this formation. The holder should place the ball on the tee as normal. The kicker should swing his leg and follow through, but should not make contact with the ball, rather his foot should pass by its side. The holder should then roll out and pass to his back who has faded away from the line.

## Kick Off Return Team *(Fig 94)*

The rules state that there must be five players between ten and fifteen yards from the kick-off line. It is usual to use the five interior linemen in this position. As the ball is kicked they check to see if it is an onside (short) kick. If it is, they attempt to recover it. If not, they turn and sprint back fifteen yards and set up a

*Fig 93  British International Steve Raven (23) waits for the ball to be placed on the tee before he attempts a 38-yard field goal.*

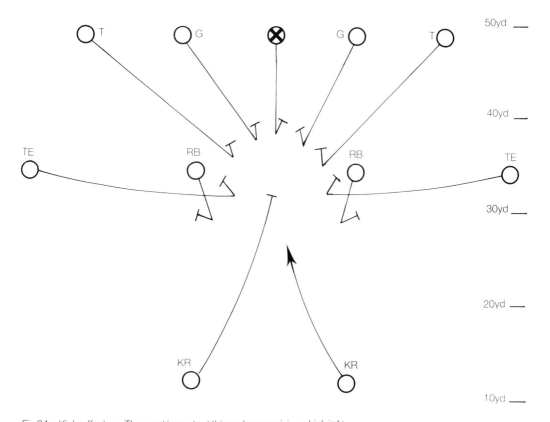

*Fig 94  Kick-off return. The most important thing when receiving a kick is to gain possession.*

# Offensive Game

wedge as quickly as possible. The returner who catches the ball should shout 'go' as he enters the wedge, and the whole team races up-field. Remember to block high – it is illegal on kick-offs to block below the waist, so don't give away needless penalties.

This is a description of a middle return, but you can design left and right returns on a similar basis.

# 6 Defensive Game

## DEFENSIVE GAME PLAN

'Getting there fastest with the mostest', is how one coach described his offensive philosophy. This maxim could equally be applied to defense, the difference being that on defense you do not know where 'there' is. Whilst offense is all about action, defense is all about reaction. The aim of the defense is quite simple – to get as many men to the ball carrier as quickly as possible.

## Huddle

Like the offense, the defense will huddle before each play. One player (usually a middle linebacker) is appointed as the defensive captain and will inform the defense what their assignments will be for the next down. Defensive play calls are not dissimilar to the offensive calls. They usually consist of the formation, the pass coverage, and any special assignments, such as linebackers blitzing.

The defense will huddle immediately behind the ball and should break from the huddle well before the offense do so. The linemen and corner backs move immediately to their positions. It is usual for linebackers and safeties to line up over the strong side of the offense. One defender is appointed to call the strong side, which is usually the side of the tight end, and he should shout loudly 'strong left' (or right) as the offense lines up. The remaining defenders should then move quickly to their positions.

## Formations

There are as many defensive formations as there are offensive ones, and your choice will depend on many things. If you are playing a *pressure* defense, to force the offense into errors, you will choose a formation which employs more linemen and linebackers and fewer defensive backs. If you are trying to *contain* the offense, just to prevent them gaining yards, you would use a line-up which had extra men in the secondary. However, it is important to remember that a defensive formation is merely a means to an end and your reaction is more important than your alignment. It is not where you line up, it is where you finish up.

Defensive formations are normally referred to by numbers. A 43 defense would consist of four down linemen, three linebackers and four defensive backs. The trend is to state the number of men on the line, with the number of linebackers, and to assume people can calculate the number of men in the secondary. As with the offense, your coach may use different names for the given formations.

## 52 *(Fig 95)*

This is one of the most common defenses used in the NFL. It features three linemen and four linebackers, but is called the 52 because the two outside linebackers are up on the line. The two middle backers are anything between one-and-a-half and five yards deep.

This is an excellent general purpose defense. The four men in the secondary provide deep coverage against the pass. The line-

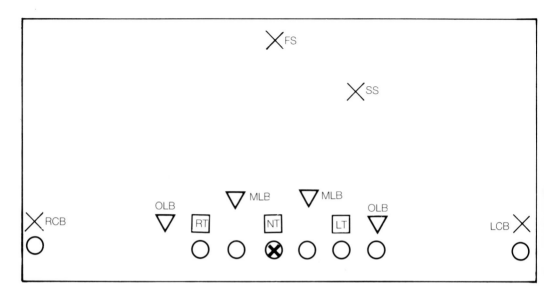

Fig 95   52 – strong left.

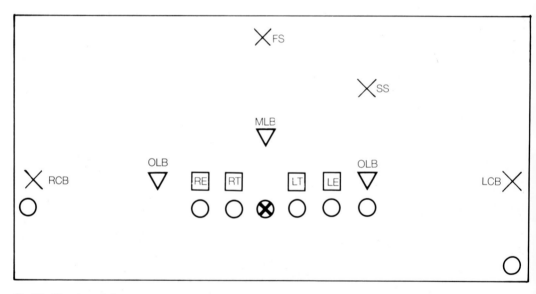

Fig 96   61 – strong left.

backers can vary their assignments by blitzing or stunting and this allows the formation to be equally good for pressuring or containing the offense. Its main weakness is on either side of the nose tackle. If you play this defense the nose tackle must be your fastest and most able lineman.

## 61 *(Fig 96)*

The 61 is a variation of the 52. It removes the problem of the weakness around the nose tackle but places an even greater responsibility on the sole middle linebacker who has to cover a large area of field. With four linemen you can mount a strong pass rush, but the surprise element of blitzing linebackers is balanced by a weakening of the pass coverage.

## 53 *(Fig 98)*

Although pro teams prefer the seven-man front, with its all round capabilities, college and high school teams often use an eight-man front which is more effective against the run. The 53 defense is an eight-man version of the 52. A fifth linebacker is added to support the nose tackle. The strong outside linebacker lines up outside the tight end. The tackles line up just outside their offensive counterparts.

## 62 *(Fig 99)*

The 62 is an eight-man version of the 61. A second middle linebacker is added to reinforce the lateral coverage of wide runs. The four linemen often line up in the gaps and this makes the 62 very strong against middle runs as well. Its main weakness is against off-tackle runs, when the offense has good blocking angles against the defensive linemen.

## 52-Monster

The 52-Monster defense is half-way between a seven-man front and an eight-man front.

Fig 97   Defense means 'getting there fastest with the mostest', as Walter
        Payton discovers to his cost.

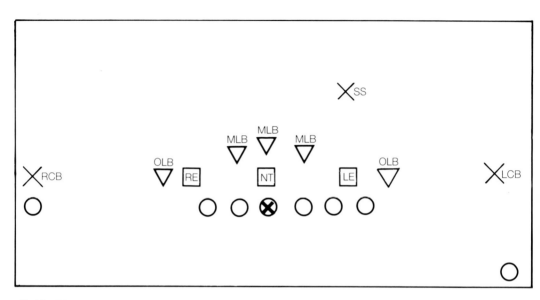

*Fig 98    53 – strong left.*

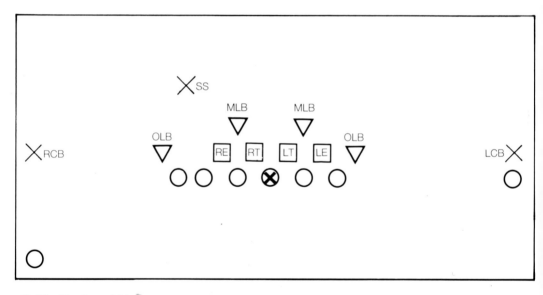

*Fig 99    62 – strong right.*

The free safety is given a totally free role in this formation. He is designated the 'monster man' (sometimes called a 'rover'). He will choose his alignment according to the offensive formation, and on the down and distance to go. On third and long he will probably drop back into the secondary, whilst on second and one he may well move up to support the strong outside linebacker. This is a very versatile defense but it needs an experienced and capable player as your monster man.

## 42-Nickel *(Fig 100)*

On certain downs, the defense may well move into a nickel formation. With its five defensive backs this is very strong against the pass. Obviously it is weak against the run, but on third and twenty it should be able to stop the first down.

## Gap-8 *(Fig 101)*

The Gap-8 is a form of goal-line defense. Within your 10-yard line you cannot afford to play a containing defense. You must attack the offense and force the error. Eight players line up in the gaps and charge into the backfield. It is essential that any receivers are detained on the line of scrimmage as this defense is weak against the aerial attack.

## Stunts *(Fig 102)*

A stunt on defense is similar to a cross block on offense in that two or more defenders exchange assignments. This can prevent double teaming by the offense and also cause them to miss blocks. The disadvantage of stunting is that it causes problems with pursuit, as defenders often get in each other's way.

It is best to use a stunt only as an occasional weapon. If you stunt too often, the offense will delay for a second and pick up the stunting men. The failure of a stunt will often leave gaping holes in the defense, but if it works you can make the big play.

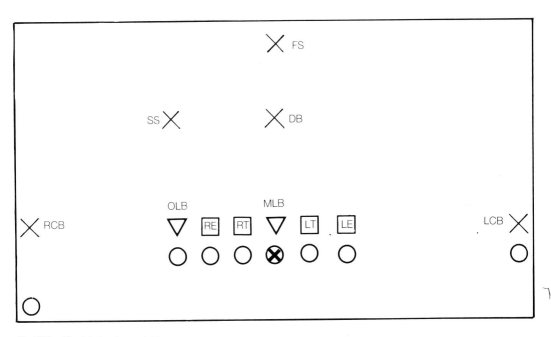

Fig 100    42-nickel – strong right.

# Defensive Game

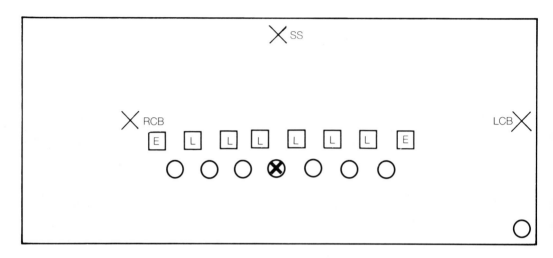

Fig 101   Gap-8.

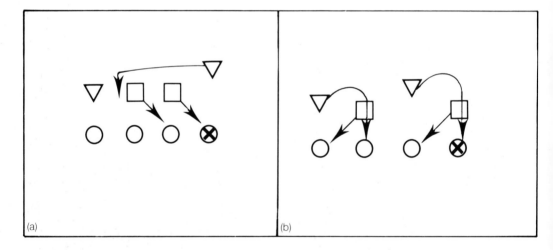

Fig 102   Stunts: (a) half line slant – the two defensive linemen slant inwards and the lone middle backer takes a long fast run round the outside; (b) loop manoeuvre – each defensive lineman slants outside and the linebacker loops behind him.

## DEFENDING THE RUN

When discussing the offense we said that running the ball is the safest way to advance down the field. From this statement it is ob-vious that the defense's first aim must be to prevent the run and force the offense into passing. If you are unable to stop the run, the offense can just take four or five yards at a time and grind their way into the endzone.

Stopping the run is not as easy as it sounds. The initial reaction of newcomers to the game is to watch for the snap and charge in on the ball carrier. Unfortunately, if the offense runs a counter or misdirection play, then you can be made to look very silly indeed. To play a successful defense against the run you must work as a unit. Everybody has a job to do and you must make sure you do your job before closing in on the ball. This is called 'staying home'. Don't commit yourself until you know what the play is – you should have a good knowledge of the sort of plays that offenses generally run, then you can adjust your own play to counteract them.

As with all the assignments given in this book, your coach may tell you that he wants you to react differently, but in the absence of any other instructions, the following is a good guide to defensive play.

## Linemen

The defensive linemen can be considered in two groups: the defensive ends, who usually line up opposite the offensive tackles, and the defensive tackles who line up inside the ends. They have different responsibilities and different assignments, although their basic techniques are the same.

Fig 103    Textbook tackling is not always possible, but you must make every effort to stop your opponent.

# Defensive Game

### The Defensive Ends (Fig 104)

As defensive end, your responsibility will be the off-tackle hole as the outside linebacker will normally line up outside the tight end. Your initial action must be to charge into the tackle and fight the pressure. If the tackle tries to drive block you out, move inside. If the tackle tries to force you in, move out to the off-tackle hole. If the tackle slants in on the inside defender, you should move into the vacant hole but watch for a trap. You should not charge over the line because a pulling guard has probably been assigned to block you. Stay at home and pick off any blocker who comes to you.

If the tight end slants in on you, or the tackle and tight end double team you, spin out and protect the off-tackle hole. If the tackle pass blocks, head for the quarterback. Your coach will tell you whether to charge outside or inside. He may also give you responsibility for stopping a draw play. If he does, you must key the backs as well as the quarterback.

### The Defensive Tackles (Fig 105)

The defensive tackles line up inside the ends. If there are two tackles they are usually over the guards. If there is only one, he lines up over

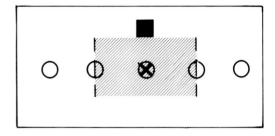

Fig 105    Nose tackle – main area of responsibility.

the center and is known as the nose tackle. This is a very difficult position to play as you must cover the whole area between the guards.

If a guard slants in on you, spin out and cover your area on that side. If the center pass blocks, charge the quarterback. You will almost certainly have responsibility for stopping a draw play so you should also keep an eye on the running backs.

To vary the line play, you may be given gap or slant assignments. On a gap play, all linemen line up in the gaps between the offensive linemen, as shown in *Fig 106*. They charge low and hard aiming to get deep into the backfield to stop the run at its source. On a slant play, each lineman will charge at the offensive lineman on his right (or left) and fight pressure, as in *Fig 107*.

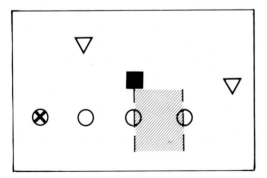

Fig 104    Defensive end – main area of responsibility.

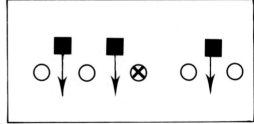

Fig 106    Gap.

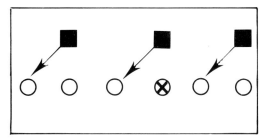

Fig 107   Slant right.

## Outside Linebackers
### *(Figs 108 & 109)*

The outside linebackers line up outside the tight end if there is one, or wide of the offensive tackle if there is no tight end. Their area of responsibility runs from the off-tackle hole all the way to the near sideline.

On outside runs to your side you will have outside containment responsibility. Force the play in so your linemen and middle backers can make the tackle. It is a selfless task but crucial to the success of any defense. Your key will be the tail back in the I-formation, or the nearest back in any other line up. If there is a tight end on your side, then you must watch your key through the tight end.

If the tight end blocks out, cover the off-tackle hole but also watch for a play action pass developing. If the tight end blocks in,

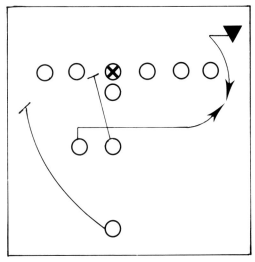

Fig 109   Flow away – outside backer keys far back.

scrape outside and force the play in. If the quarterback runs, tackle him at the line of scrimmage.

If the tight end slants in on the tackle, move into the hole and watch for backs or pulling guards. Force the play in. You must not penetrate too far or you will be susceptible to a trap block.

If the flow of the play is away from you, scrape behind your linemen but key the far back and watch for a counter or reverse. If these do not develop, pursue the play behind the line. If the play comes back towards you, you must readjust and meet the runner.

If there is no tight end over you, you should turn in all plays that either go outside or straight at you. Meet any blockers and shed them inside. If the quarterback runs with the ball, you should reach him at the line of scrimmage.

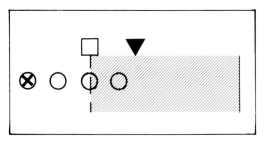

Fig 108   Outside linebacker – area of responsibility.

## Middle Linebackers
*(Figs 110 to 115)*

In pro football, the middle linebackers line up four to five yards off the line of scrimmage. In junior football, I would recommend that you are no further than two yards off. On the snap of the ball you should take a step forwards with your outside foot. This will give you momentum if the play is straight at you. Attack any blockers that come at you and force them away. Junior teams usually have two middle linebackers, who must cover the area from the center to the tackle, their keys being the full back and the football.

If the football comes through your hole, meet the blockers and turn the play inside. If the ball comes inside, away from you, move quickly across and attack the ball carrier. If the ball goes outside on your side, scrape along the line and attack the ball carrier. If it is the quarterback who carries, get outside him and take the pitch-out man on the line of scrimmage.

If the ball goes wide away from you, take deepish lateral pursuit, remaining inside the ball carrier. Key the far back, watching for a counter play and adjust your run if necessary. If the guard slants in, fill the hole and watch for a trap.

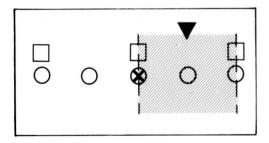

Fig 110   Middle backer – main area of responsibility.

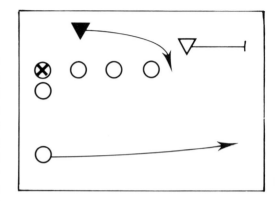

Fig 111   Scraping the line on outside play.

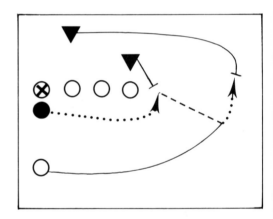

Fig 112   Linebacker play on quarterback option.

## Blitzing *(Fig 116)*

Linebackers are sometimes asked to blitz (or 'fire' or 'dog'). This means forget your usual assignments – just charge into the backfield and do as much damage as you can. Blitzing is ninety-nine per cent determination and only one per cent skill. It is the most enjoyable part of linebacker play and a coach usually has problems *stopping* his linebackers blitzing. Obviously its main problem is lack of down-field back-up. If all the linebackers blitz and the

Fig 113   Mickey Sutton – the Rams' defensive back.

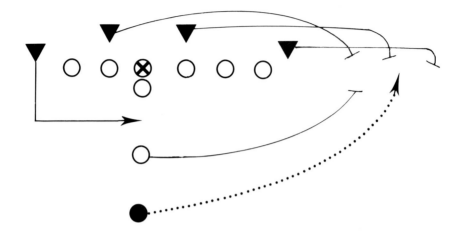

*Fig 114   Linebacker play on wide play.*

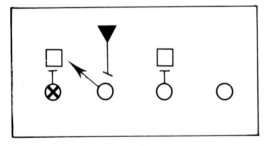

*Fig 115   Guard slants and middle backer fills hole.*

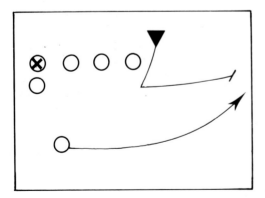

*Fig 116   Blitzing outside linebacker covers screen pass.*

offense breaks through, then you could be in big trouble.

If you are playing either outside linebacker position, you must key the nearest back as you blitz. Offenses will counteract the blitz by sending a back outside and using a screen pass to get the ball out to him. Fire in hard but if that back moves away, go with him. Take the easy option away from the offense and your blitz has more chance of success. Remember the golden rule: never let an opponent cross your path.

## Secondary *(Fig 117)*

Your responsibilities for stopping the run will be assigned by your coach. Playing in the secondary, your main responsibility is the pass but you can't spend the whole game dropping deep while the offense picks up four or five yards by running at you. On the other hand you can't get drawn in by a fake hand-off and see a bomb pass flying over your head.

Key the guard and tackle on your side. If they fire over the line of scrimmage, move in for the run. The cornerbacks are often given outside containment responsibilities on wide runs, or this job could go to the safety with the cornerback switching inside.

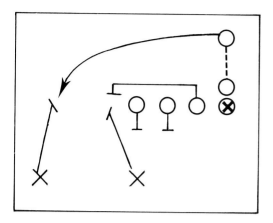

Fig 117  *Secondary keys guard and tackle and reads sweep.*

# DEFENDING THE PASS

Passing the football is much more difficult than running with it – most junior teams use the pass only as an occasional alternative to the run. However, it would be foolhardy to concentrate solely on stopping the run, as a successful pass is likely to bring a long gain and even one completion in a game can upset the defense. A slight hesitation at the snap will let the offense's running game through.

Defending the pass has one big similarity with defending the run: you must work as a team. Everybody has a job to do and you must stick to your assignment. If you are playing man-to-man and your opponent doesn't run a route then look around and help your team-mates. If nobody enters your zone, go to help someone else. Above all, talk to each other. Let everybody know if you have two or more receivers to cover. Tell your team-mate if a receiver has sneaked unnoticed into his zone.

## Linemen

The lineman's assignment on a pass is the simplest, being to charge the quarterback and stop him making the pass. You may either tackle the quarterback or bat the throw down. When you tackle him, hit high and wrap your arms around him. A quarterback ready to throw does not have a very secure grip on the ball and a good hard hit could easily cause a fumble.

Remember to watch for a draw play. Your coach will tell you if you have responsibility for stopping the draw, but it is usually the job of one or both of the defensive tackles.

## Man-to-Man Coverage
*(Figs 118 to 122)*

Man-to-man coverage is simple in theory, but difficult in execution. There are usually five eligible receivers on the offense and each of these is assigned to a defender who has to stick with him wherever he goes. This type of defense will match a running back with a linebacker and there are not many linebackers who can stick with a half back for more than fifteen or twenty yards. Man-to-man is used either as an occasional alternative to the zone, or within the defense's 20-yard line when long sprints are not going to occur. Two systems of man coverage are discussed here, although you or your coach may design many more.

### Man-1 Coverage (Fig 118)

On man-1 coverage the weak side corner-back marks the split end. The strong side cornerback takes the flankerback if there is one, or the nearest half back. The strong side middle backer covers the full back and the strong safety covers the tight end. This leaves the free safety to act much as a sweeper would in soccer. He surveys the whole situation and picks up any receiver who breaks open. The two remaining backers can either be told to blitz the quarterback or be assigned as double coverage on a particularly danger-ous receiver.

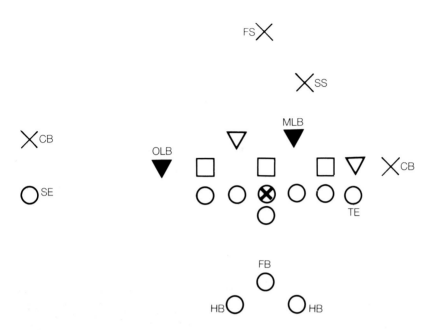

*Fig 118    Man-1 coverage versus triple back offense.*

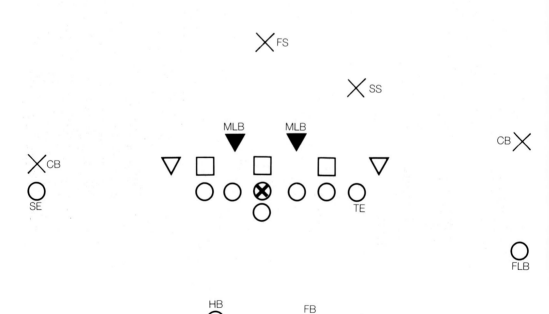

*Fig 119    Man-2 coverage versus twin back offense.*

## Man-2 Coverage (Fig 119)

On man-2 coverage, the two outside backers are released to attack the quarterback. The cornerbacks and strong safety have the same assignments as on man-1. The two middle backers pick up the full back and weak side half back, or the nearest back if there are only two in the backfield.

When running man-to-man coverage you should keep the wide receivers on the flanks by staying just inside them. Make it difficult for them to cut inside and give the quarterback the longer, tougher pass. This is called covering 'inside out'.

If both receivers are on the same side, the two cornerbacks should play a semi-zone coverage. The outside cornerback should cover the receiver who breaks outside and the inside cornerback covers the receiver who cuts inwards. If the offense uses motion, the defender assigned to the motion man should move laterally along the field to cover him (*Fig 122*).

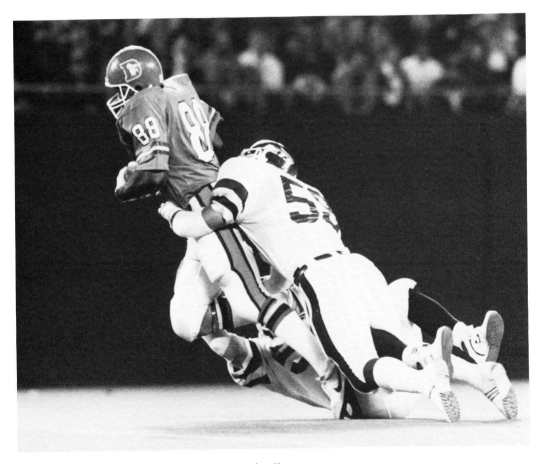

Fig 120    Tackling from behind – wrap your arms round and hang on.

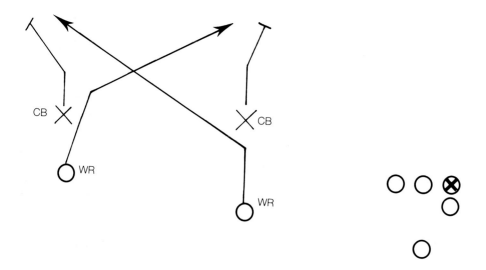

Fig 121    *Two receivers on one side – play zone on that side.*

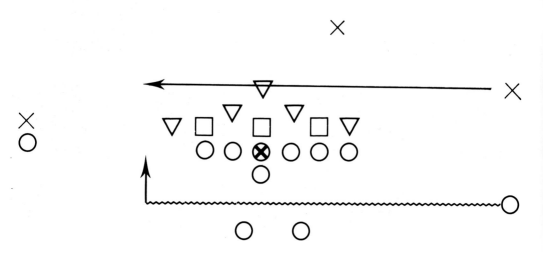

Fig 122    *Man-to-man versus motion.*

## Zone Coverage
*(Figs 123 to 125)*

Two types of zone are discussed here: a good all-round zone for general use and a prevent zone designed to stop the long bomb but at the expense of a shorter pass.

On the basic zone shown in *Fig 123* there are three deep zones and four short zones. The four short zones are between seven and eight yards off the line, with the outside men seven yards from the sidelines. The depth of the three other zones depends on down, distance and field position and can be anything from twelve yards off the line.

At certain times during a game you will be prepared to allow the offense a short pass or even a first down, as long as you do not concede a touchdown. This is when you are leading near the end of a half or a game and you are sure the offense will pass. To achieve this, use a coverage called a prevent zone (*Fig 124*). (This is pronounced *pre*-vent with the accent on the first syllable.) The three deep-zone defenders line up twelve to fifteen yards off the line of scrimmage, keeping all receivers in front of them. Two fast defenders are assigned to the wide receivers and the strong outside linebacker covers the tight end. They cover these players man-to-man within ten yards of the line and then move to their zones if their opponent goes deep. The weak backer covers the nearest back man-to-man if he runs a route, otherwise he drops to his short zone.

In zone defense, motion by the offense is

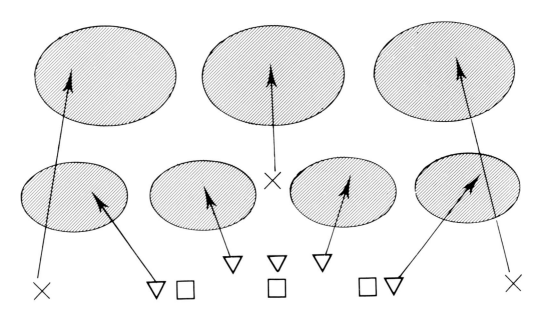

Fig 123   *Zone coverage – defenders cover an area or zone rather than an individual receiver.*

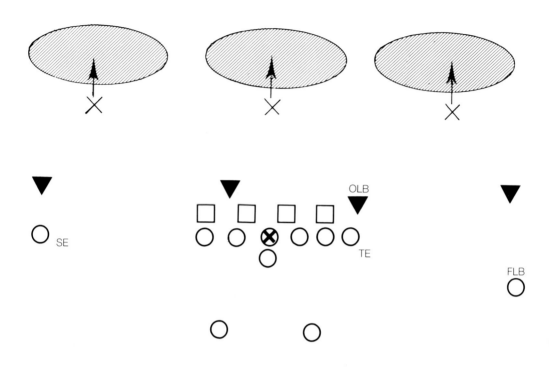

Fig 124   Prevent zone. This coverage is only used to stop a very long pass.

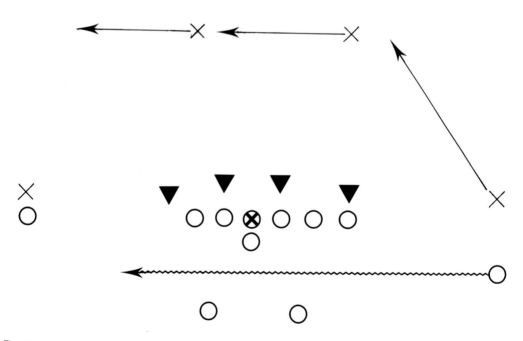

Fig 125   Rotating zones to cover offensive motion.

countered by rotating the zones. *Fig 125* shows how the flankerback's motion is covered by two deep defenders moving with him and the outside linebacker dropping into a deeper position. The zones can also be rotated if the quarterback rolls out to one side before passing. The nearer he goes to one sideline, the less the need to cover the other side of the field.

## SPECIAL TEAMS ON DEFENSE

As with the offensive special teams, the kick-off team, the punt return team and the goal-kick defense are no place for the faint hearted. Here you have to hustle, chase and hit as hard as you can. Any lack of effort will result in a score or good field position for the opposition.

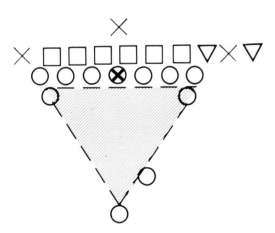

*Fig 126    Goal-kick defense. The defenders' aim is to get into the triangle and block the kick.*

## Goal-Kick *(Fig 126)*

This could be called a gap-6 defense. Six down linemen are positioned in the gaps of the offensive line. Two linebackers are put to one side or the other to overload part of the line. These eight men have the single aim of breaking into the triangle and blocking the kick. The two cornerbacks line up just outside the line and the safety stands three yards behind. Their first responsibility is to stop any passing play that the offense may run off a fake kick.

## Kick-Off *(Fig 127)*

The first thing a kick-off team needs is a kicker who can put the ball into the endzone, so that the offense will have to start their drive from the 20-yard line. Most kick-off returns are around twenty yards so any kick that is short will probably be moved out beyond the 20-yard line.

The kick-off team has five players on either side of the kicker. There should be about five yards between each person and about five yards between the players and the ball. The players are numbered L1 to L5 on the left and R1 to R5 on the right. As the kicker runs up to kick off, the rest of the team start to move but must remain behind the ball until it is kicked.

The two outside players (L5 and R5) head straight for the ball carrier. They must avoid being blocked and aim to tackle as soon as possible. The eight other men face down field to provide coverage over the whole pitch. They should run straight for fifteen yards and then move towards the returner. They should still maintain their position in the line and not cross in front of or behind their team-mates. Players L4 and R4 have outside containment duties and should stay outside the return man. L1 and R1 are the *wedge-busters*. They must

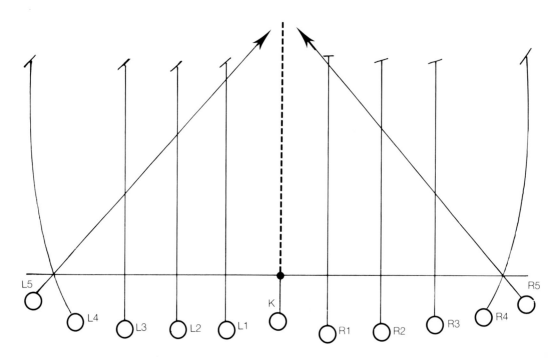

Fig 127   Kick-off. The kick-off team must run at top speed to retain the returner down-field.

take on the returning blockers and create gaps for their team-mates to attack the ball. The kicker should trail the play and act as safety. The kick-off team must go at full speed until the whistle sounds to end the play. Never assume that the ball will not be returned even if it does go into the endzone. If you are blocked on your way down, *quickly* return to your position in the line.

### Onside Kick (Fig 128)

If you are desperate for possession of the ball after the kick-off and are prepared to risk poor field position if you don't recover it, then you must try the onside kick. This is a kick which is similar to the Rugby Union kick-off. The ball is kicked at an angle so that it would cross the

sideline about fifteen yards down-field. The kick-off team overloads that side of the field and chases hard. After the ball has gone ten yards the nearest man to it should attempt to recover it, whilst the other players block the return team. In these circumstances, do not attempt to advance the ball yourself, rather you should fall on the ball and let your offensive unit take over.

## Punt Return *(Figs 129 & 131)*

The punt return team can have two different assignments: either you can attack the punter or you can opt to return the kick. You should adopt a formation which allows you to carry out both of these options as well as defending a run or a pass. In the formation shown in *Fig*

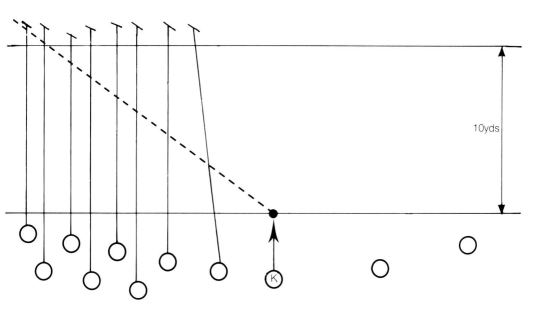

Fig 128    The onside kick-off is similar to the rugby football kick-off.

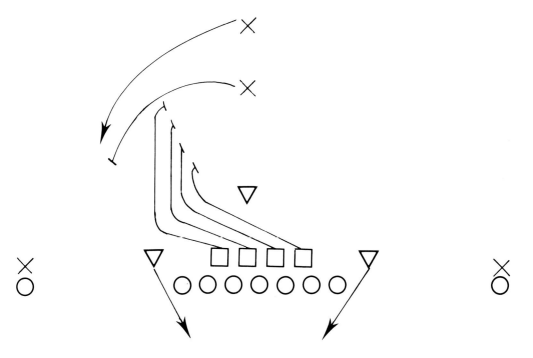

Fig 129    Punt return formation – only two players attack the punter.

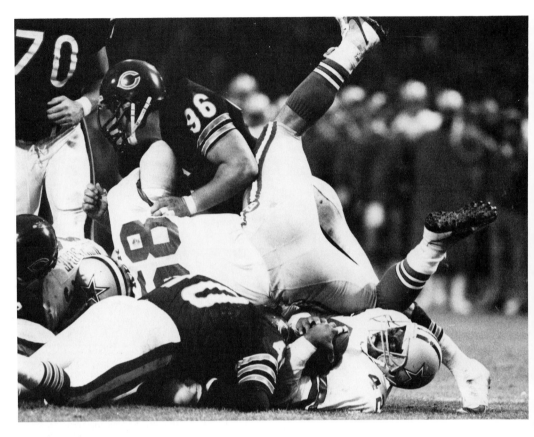

Fig 130   Some unorthodox tackling!

*129*, there are six men on the line. The two end men always go after the punter. The four interior men can either attack the punter or peel off to form a wall for the return man to run behind. All players who attack the punter should be aiming for a point four-and-a-half yards in front of where he lines up. Their aim is to charge down the punt and this is the point where contact is made. It allows the punter to take two paces forwards and swing his leg which should make contact with the ball just as the defense players reach him.

The two cornerbacks should cover the wide-outs and block them all the way down the field. These players are allowed to leave the line at the snap so it is important to slow their progress as much as possible. The middle backer stands six yards off the line, ready to stop any attempt at a run. Once the ball is kicked he should drop back and block for the returner.

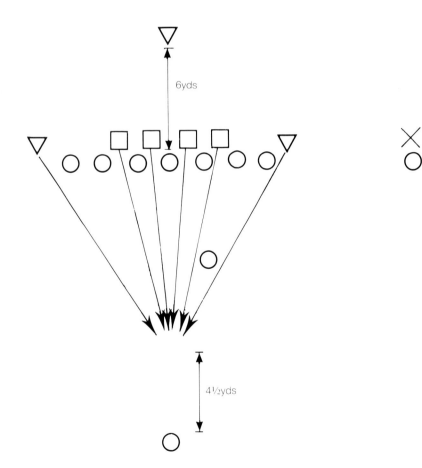

Fig 131  Attacking the punter. The defense aims at a point just in front
         of the punter.

# 7 Coaching

The head coach of a team in the United States will more than likely have an army of assistants – assistant coaches, scouts and statisticians are all on hand to make the job easier. As a coach in Britain it is quite possible that you will have to do most of these jobs yourself. Coaching a team is not just standing on the sidelines, sending in the plays – it is organising and leading the practice schedules; it is watching opposing teams and finding their strengths and weaknesses; most important of all, it is getting the best out of your players.

## PRACTICE

While British athletes go 'training', Americans talk about going to 'practice'. The difference is quite simple – if you go soccer 'training' then you will spend half the time on fitness work and the other half split between techniques and tactics. The American philosophy is to work on personal fitness in your own time and to reserve practice sessions for the skills and strategies specific to your sport. This ideal is pertinent to American football in Britain where time allotted to practice is usually only a few hours a week. As a coach you do not want to spend time covering things that players are capable of doing on their own. You should encourage the team to go road running and weight-training outside the practice session. Then you can use your valuable time to its best advantage.

The football season in Britain lasts only four months, from the end of April to the end of August. Pre-season games are usually played during April giving a five-month period of game readiness. For two months before this you should concentrate on learning plays and formations and on executing assignments correctly. The two months before that are allocated to the basics of the game: blocking, tackling, passing and running. Therefore your practice sessions cover a nine-month period, divided into three distinct sections.

During the first two months, a typical three-hour practice session could look something like this:

| | |
|---|---|
| 10:00–10:30 | Warm-up, stretching, agilities. |
| 10:30–11:00 | Line techniques – stances, blocking, pulling, jam and shed, etc. |
| 11:00–11:30 | Offensive backfield techniques – stances, passing, catching, carrying, etc. |
| 11:30–12:00 | Defensive techniques – stances, zones, man-to-man, tackling. |
| 12:00–12:30 | Scrimmage (no tackling, two-hand touch). |
| 12:30– 1:00 | Sprints and cool down. |

If you have a large squad and enough coaches, it would be better to divide the players into three groups and rotate them through the techniques sessions:

| | Group 1 | Group 2 | Group 3 |
|---|---|---|---|
| 10:00–10:30 | Line | Defense | Offense |
| 11:00–11:30 | Offense | Line | Defense |
| 11:30–12:00 | Defense | Offense | Line |

The scrimmage session is used to get the players acting as a team. There is no need for complexity and the offense needs to know only a handful of plays. The defense should keep to two favourite formations and concentrate on making them work. The main aim of

Fig 132 Sam Clapham, San Diego offensive tackle, in a three-point stance.

these early training sessions is to develop the individual skills of the players and to assign players to the positions in which they will be the best asset to the team.

The pre-season practices are to enlarge the repertoire of your units and to improve their execution. Players will still spend time on basic techniques but only those which are specific to their allotted position. Each player should be given a play book which they will have to learn by heart. Then each new play or formation can be introduced gradually over the two-month period until all are known and understood.

| | |
|---|---|
| 10:00–10:30 | Warm-up, stretching, agilities. |
| 10:30–11:30 | Offense and defense split into their units and practise techniques and plays. |
| 11:30–12:00 | Scrimmage. |
| 12:00–12:30 | Special teams – kick-off, punt, field goal (non contact). |
| 12:30– 1:00 | Sprints and cool down. |

A week before your first game you should change to your in-season practice schedule. This concentrates on the execution of plays and defenses that you hope will work against your forthcoming opponents.

| | |
|---|---|
| 10:00–10:30 | Warm-up, stretching, agilities. |
| 10:30–12:00 | Offense and defense work in their units. They practise techniques and any special plays designed for the next game. |
| 12:00–12:10 | Kick-off and kick-off return (non contact). |
| 12:10–12:20 | Punt and punt return (non contact). |
| 12:20–12:30 | Field goal. |
| 12:30– 1:00 | Sprints and cool down. |

In discussing all these practice schedules it is important to be flexible. If you feel that a specific aspect of your game needs more time, rearrange the schedule to accommodate this. This is especially so during pre-season training when you should not move on to a new play or formation until you are sure the players have absorbed the current ones.

Notice that relatively little time is spent on full contact scrimmage. There are two reasons for this: you cannot see everything that is going on during scrimmage so players will develop bad habits which are difficult to correct, and injuries will be sustained which could leave your best players on the sidelines.

# SCOUTING

Whenever possible, you should go and watch your opponents playing. Although you probably do not have the resources to take a detailed analysis of a game, there are several things you can pick up and use in your practice schedules. I usually take a list of the points I want to note with me and fill it in during and immediately after the game.

## Scouting List

### Offense

Two favourite formations
Two best running plays
Best passing play
Best ball carrier
Best receiver
Ratio of passing to running
What plays must we stop to beat them?
What do they do on goal-line?
Do they go for one or two extra points?
What abilities and faults does the quarterback have?

### Defense

Two favourite formations
Do they stunt?

Fig 133    Keep the ball tucked away.

Do they shift formations?
Do they contain or pressurise?
Which linebackers blitz?
Zone or man-to-man?
What do they do on goal-line?
Where are they weak?

### Special Teams

Punter's shirt number
What punt formation do they use?
What distance do they punt?
What punt returns do they use?
What distance do they kick-off?
What is their field goal range?
Do they run or pass from field goal or punt formations?

You should also make notes about anything that catches your eye during the game. Do they run any gimmick plays (reverses, etc)? Does a particular back fumble the ball often? Does a certain linebacker over-react to offensive motion? Always write everything down as it is easy to forget later.

Use this information in your practice sessions. Inform your players about the opposition and what they can and cannot do well. And allow for the fact that your opponents may have changed everything by the time you come to play them!

## The Game

During a game you will have to make decisions on your team tactics. Some coaches call every play for offense and defense. Others discuss the general plan with their quarterback or defensive captain and then allow the player to call the play, sending in specific plays from the sideline when needed. Although the

call for a specific play depends on many circumstances such as down, distance, field position and game time, there are some rules which can help you make your decisions. For offensive play:

1.  On first down, go for a touchdown.
2.  On third down, go for a first down.
3.  If you are just in front in the fourth quarter, keep the ball on the ground, not in the air.
4.  Take the weather into consideration. It is difficult to pass into a strong wind or to sweep on a wet muddy field.
5.  Don't gamble unless you are well in front or you are losing and running out of time.
6.  When you get within twenty yards of their endzone, remember how you got there.
7.  If something works, stick with it.

The defense has rules which are very similar to the offense's rules:

1.  Don't gamble if you are in front.
2.  When the offense is within twenty yards of your endzone, remember how they got there.
3.  Always be ready for anything.
4.  Think like a quarterback. What plays would you call against your defense?

And, as with all 'rules' of this type, be prepared to forget them all! Sometimes you just get a feeling for the right play call. Sometimes you will be wrong, but a good coach is correct more often than not.

Football is a very simple game. If the offense runs simple plays then there is less chance of mistake – often the winning team is the one that makes the fewest errors. Competent execution of basic plays by all units of a team is the foundation of a winning side.

# Glossary

**Assignment**  A player's exact action or reaction on any given play.

**Audible**  A play called at the line of scrimmage. The quarterback will audible if he feels that the defense's alignment necessitates a change to the play called in the huddle.

**Base Position**  Also called the hitting position, the two point stance or the linebacker stance, this crouched position is the most basic of all techniques.

**Black Cap**  A nickname given to the head official, who wears a black cap. (Other officials wear white hats.)

**Blitz**  A move in which linebackers and defensive backs abandon their normal defensive assignments and attack the quarterback.

**Blocking**  Preventing a defender from reaching the ball carrier by legally obstructing him.

**Bomb**  A long forward pass.

**Bump and Run**  A technique used against receivers which involves delaying their passage down-field.

**Cheating**  A player is said to be 'cheating' when he attempts to make his assignment easier and ends up letting the opposition know what he intends to do. For example, a guard may lean in the direction he is going to pull, or a blitzing linebacker may line up closer to the line of scrimmage.

**Clipping**  An illegal block. Clipping is making contact with a defender from the side or from behind.

**Counter**  A misdirection run by the half back off a fake to the full back.

**Coverage**  The movement of linebackers and defensive backs to prevent completion of a pass.

**Cut Block**  A block used to bring an opponent down.

**Cut**  The sudden change of direction by a runner or receiver.

**Dive**  A running play where the ball carrier has no lead blockers.

**Dog**  Same as blitz.

**Draw**  A running play designed to look like a pass.

**Fire**  Same as blitz.

**Flag**  A pass route where the receiver cuts outwards towards the corner flag.

**Fly**  A pass route where the receiver attempts to beat the defender by speed alone.

**Fumble**  To drop the ball after previously being in possession.

# Glossary

**Game Plan**  The plays and formations a coach thinks will work against the next opponents.

**Gap**  The space between men on the offensive line.

**Hand-off**  The means of transferring the football from the quarterback to a running back.

**Holding**  The act of illegally grabbing an opponent. Offensive players are *not* allowed to grasp or encircle defenders with their hands and arms. Defensive players *are* allowed to grasp, but only to remove a blocker from their path. They cannot hold a blocker to prevent him leaving the area.

**Hole**  A numbered gap in the offensive line, or a gap in the defense forced open by offensive blockers.

**Honest**  A player is said to be 'honest' if he does not anticipate his opponent's action, or does not make his own actions obvious to the opposition (see also Cheating).

**Hook**  A pass route where the receiver runs out and then curls back sharply towards the line of scrimmage.

**In**  A pass route where the receiver cuts in towards centre field.

**Inside**  The area of the offensive line between the tackles.

**Interference**  Blockers leading the ball carrier are said to be running interference.

**Key**  A member of the opposing side a defender watches in order to decide on his actions.

**Man-to-Man**  A type of pass coverage where each receiver is assigned an individual defender.

**Monster**  A linebacker who is given a free role.

**Motion**  Immediately prior to the snap, all members of the offense must be stationary, with the exception of one man who may move parallel to the line of scrimmage. This man is said to be 'in motion'.

**Moves**  A player with the ability to jink past defenders or to change direction quickly is said to have good 'moves'.

**Onside Kick**  A short kick-off where the kicking team attempts to regain possession.

**Option**  Any play where the ball carrier has different choices depending on the reaction of the defense.

**Out**  A pass route where the receiver cuts out towards the side line.

**Outside**  The areas of the offensive line beyond the tackles.

**Pass Pocket**  The area around a quarterback, which is protected by blockers, in which he sets up to pass.

**Pass Rush**  The charge of certain defenders (usually linemen or linebackers) who attempt to tackle the quarterback before he can pass the football.

**Pattern**  A set of routes run by the receivers.

**Pitch-out**  A rugby-style pass from the quarterback to the running back.

**Play Action**   A passing play that stems from a fake run.

**Post**   A pass route where the receiver cuts towards the goal post.

**Prevent Defense**   A defense designed to give up a first down whilst preventing a touchdown.

**Pull**   To leave the line of scrimmage and lead for a runner.

**Reverse**   A play where the runner hands off to a receiver running in the opposite direction.

**Roll Out**   A play where the quarterback moves towards the sideline before passing.

**Rover**   See monster.

**Sack**   To tackle the quarterback before he can pass the ball.

**Scramble**   The quarterback 'scrambles' when his offensive line collapses and he has to scamper about to avoid being sacked.

**Screen**   A passing play where members of the offensive line leave the pass pocket and form a screen in front of the receiver, who is usually a running back.

**Shotgun**   A formation where the quarterback stands back off the line of scrimmage.

**Slant**   A pass route where the receiver runs at a 45 degree angle to the line of scrimmage. A running play that hits at the off-tackle hole (between tackle and tight end) is also known as a slant.

**Special Team**   Any of the teams involved with kicking the football.

**Straight-arm**   To fend off a tackler by extending your arm and hitting him with your palm. (Similar to the rugby football 'hand-off'.)

**Stripping**   To remove the ball from the grasp of a runner.

**Strong Side**   The side of the offense with the tight end.

**Stunt**   A defensive play where two defenders exchange assignments.

**Sweep**   An outside run.

**Timing Pattern**   A set of routes designed to release each receiver in turn.

**Turn-over**   A change of possession due to a forced error such as a fumble or an interception.

**Turn-round**   A change of possession due to a team failing to make a first down, or kicking the ball.

**Weak Side**   The side of the offense without the tight end.

**Zone**   A type of pass coverage where each defender is allocated a region of the field to patrol.

# Useful Addresses

**British American Football Coaches Association**
10 Appleby Walk
Northampton
NN3 1PP

**British American Football Referees Association**
26 Somerville Road
Daventry
Northampton
NN11 4RT

**Junior American Football League**
6 Ryefield
Luton
Bedfordshire
LU3 4JD

**Irish American Football League**
13 Russell Avenue
East Wall
Dublin 3

**NFL Supporters Club**
Cape House
60A Priory Road
Tonbridge
Kent

# Index

# Index

# *Index*

# Crowood Sports Books

| | | |
|---|---|---|
| | **American Football** – The Skills of the Game | *Les Wilson* |
| ★ | **Badminton** – The Skills of the Game | *Peter Roper* |
| | **Basketball** – The Skills of the Game | *Paul Stimpson* |
| ★ | **Canoeing** – Skills and Techniques | *Neil Shave* |
| ★ | **The Skills of Cricket** | *Keith Andrew* |
| | **Crown Green Bowls** – The Skills of the Game | *Harry Barratt* |
| | **Endurance Running** | *Norman Brook* |
| ★ | **Fitness for Sport** | *Rex Hazeldine* |
| ★ | **Golf** – The Skills of the Game | *John Stirling* |
| | **Hockey** – The Skills of the Game | *John Cadman* |
| ★ | **Judo** – Skills and Techniques | *Tony Reay* |
| | **Jumping** | *Malcolm Arnold* |
| | **Karate** – The Skills of the Game | *Vic Charles* |
| ★ | **Rugby Union** – The Skills of the Game | *Barrie Corless* |
| ★ | **Skiing** – Developing Your Skill | *John Shedden* |
| | **Cross-Country Skiing** | *Paddy Field and Tim Walker* |
| | **Sprinting and Hurdling** | *Peter Warden* |
| ★ | **Squash** – The Skills of the Game | *Ian McKenzie* |
| | **Swimming** | *John Verrier* |
| | **Table Tennis** – The Skills of the Game | *Gordon Steggall* |
| | **Tennis** – The Skills of the Game | *Charles Applewhaite and Bill Moss* |
| | **Throwing** | *Max Jones* |
| | **Volleyball** – The Skills of the Game | *Keith Nicholls* |
| ★ | **Windsurfing** – Improving Techniques | *Ben Oakley* |

★ **Also available in paperback**

**Further details of titles available or in preparation can be obtained from the publishers.**